*Note from the translators*:
Unless otherwise indicated, we have translated the citations, some of which had already been translated into French from other languages.

*cover:*
Image of Gazira Babeli for the cover of the exhibition catalogue of Holy Fire, Art of the Digital Age, iMAL, Brussels, published by Yves Bernard and Domenico Quaranta, 2008.

*Acknowledgements:*
To my wife, Christiane Morelle, with whom I have shared the happiness every day of a journey to the end of the earth and to the very beginnings of cinema ...
To Alain Montesse, a filmmaker and academic, who was among the first to open this "Northwest Passage" and establish a link between the memory palaces and the digital arts. Without his guidance into these unknown territories, my own journey in the memory palaces could not have taken place.
To Guy Chapouillié, a movie director and founder of the ESAV in Toulouse, who supervised my doctoral dissertation upon which this essay is based, and who accompanied me in this research with vigilance, friendship, and his unshakeable optimism.
To Gazira Babeli
To Yves Bernard


1 CITÉ RIVERIN
75010 PARIS
http://www.disvoir.com

ISBN 9782914563833


PRINTED IN EUROPE

# MNEMOSYNE

## A HISTORY OF THE ARTS OF MEMORY
## FROM ANTIQUITY TO CONTEMPORARY MULTIMEDIA CREATION

FRANÇOIS BOUTONNET

*translated from French by*
CHARLES LA VIA & ADAM CLARK

see our complete catalogue at: http://www.disvoir.com

series edited by

DANIELE RIVIERE

in the same series “visual arts/ essay”

BRITISH BLACK ART
DEBATES ON WESTERN ART HISTORY

*Sophie Orlando*

THE IMAGE-MATTER
EMERGING MATERIALS AND IMAGINARY METAMORPHOSIS

*Dominique Peysson*

THE MUTANT FLESH
FABRICATION OF A POSTHUMAN

*Denis Baron*

NARRATIVITY: HOW VISUAL ARTS, CINEMA AND LITERATURE ARE TELLING THE WORLD TODAY

*René Audet, Claude Romano, Laurence Dreyfus, Carl Therrien, Hugues Marchal*

BLACK IS A COLOR: A HISTORY OF AFRICAN AMERICAN ART

*Elvan Zabunyan*

KEEP THIS SEX OUT OF MY SIGHT

*Elvan Zabunyan, Chrystel Besse, Arlette Fontan, Françoise Gaillard, Marie-Joseph Bertini*

CONTEMPORARY PRACTICES: ART AS EXPERIENCE

*Paul Ardenne, Pascal Beausse, Laurent Goumarre*

TECHNO: AN ARTISTIC AND POLITICAL LABORATORY OF THE PRESENT

*Michel Gaillot, Jean-Luc Nancy, Michel Maffesoli*

SOUND AND THE VISUAL ARTS

*Jean-Yves Bosseur*

IN FAVOUR OF TODAY’S ART

*François Dagognet*

CONTENTS

*Ars Magna*

We can think in images
since Mnemosyne
has nourished
the arts of representation
of the world
and of thinking
about the world.
The arts of memory
introduced an
excitation of thought,
which became an art,
this Ars Magna dreamed
up by Ramon Llull,
and raised up by
Giordano Bruno
to the status of the Link,
where "learning thoughts"
evolved progressively
toward "learning to think,"
and today nourishes
our digital culture.

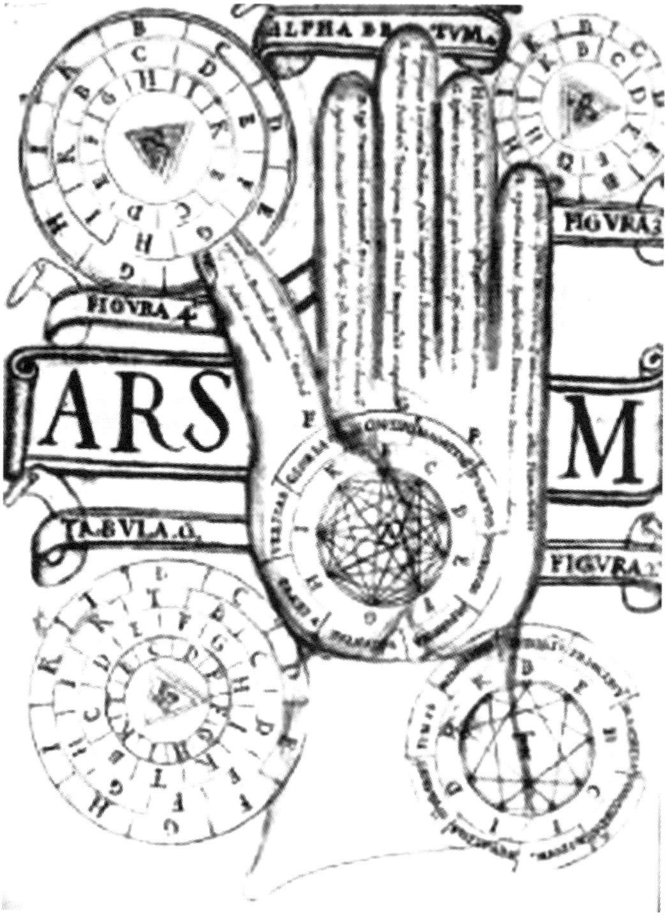


*Ars Magna* – Ramon Llull – Spain 1272

# FOREWORD

***M****nemosyne*[1] has presided over the fragile emulations between memory and creation, knowledge and poetry, and the sciences and the arts since the dawn of time. It was under her sign, twenty-seven centuries ago in Ancient Greece, that the arts of memory embarked upon a journey toward a global art by combining for the first time places and memory, space and time, representation and movement, and image and thought. It is under her sign that the various models of knowledge have unfolded over time. It is under her sign that the very idea of visual thought, or thinking in images, is placed. It was in reference to Mnemosyne that Aby Warburg, in the early twentieth century, carried out his ultimate research for a sort of theater of memory, thus bringing back to the fore the several thousand year-old inventions of the ancient arts of memory.

The myth of Mnemosyne therefore places memory at the beginning, makes it the matrix in which all human arts and knowledge are invented. While memory gathers and transmits all the traces of life in the world, it is not simply an archive and an aggregation; it is also an instrument of invention and meditation. For Frances Amelia Yates, who resurrected the arts of memory from oblivion,

[1] Mnemosyne, daughter of Gaia and Uranus, is the goddess of Memory. Her liaison with Zeus gave birth to the nine Muses - eloquence, history, poetry, music, tragedy, pantomime, dance, comedy, and astronomy. Inspired by the nine muses, placed directly under the divine breath, the poet reveals the invisible and gives meaning to the world.

> few people know that the Greeks, who invented many arts, invented an art of memory which, like their other arts, was passed on to Rome whence it descended in the European tradition. This art seeks to memorise through a technique of impressing "places" and "images" on memory. It has usually been classed as "mnemotechnics", which in modern times seems a rather unimportant branch of human activity. But in the ages before printing a trained memory was vitally important.[2]

In Antiquity, during that long period in which there was no possibility of storing thought and mechanically reproducing writing, the transmission of knowledge was essentially oral. The only form of memorization was to learn texts by heart; and this memorization functioned through a method that associated *thought* to *places* (*loci*) and *images* (*imagines*). The three principles on which this memorization technique is based are order, association, and repetition. In order to memorize them, ideas and texts were linked to stages in a mental itinerary in a place meticulously memorized beforehand. The thought-place link was sealed by implanting in this place a mental image of a striking scene, like statues in a palace. The thought elements thus stored could be retrieved by an orderly *walk* through the palace of memory. The hypothesis of such a process can already be found in the work of Plato, for whom images *speak* more directly to the soul, and are therefore better vectors of memorization.

This link between *thought*, *places,* and *images* is the first human technique invented for gathering and organizing memory. Because of the status it confers upon places and images, it is astonishingly modern. For the first time, the hypothesis of a mental

[2] Frances Amelia Yates, *The Art of Memory,* (London: Routledge and Kegan Paul, 1966).

landscape is posited: the place becomes a human creation, which can no longer be separated from the place. Ideas are expressed in a new way explicitly by images, and these images are no longer pure evanescence, but tools in the exercise of thinking. The phantasmagorical visions that populate imaginary architectures are felt by those experiencing them as suitable for imprinting in memory the thread of their thoughts. As if the image, inseparable from placing thoughts in memory, were weaving the fabric of memory itself. What the arts of memory reveal to us about the link between *thought*, *places,* and *images*, is the important function of *walking* through an *imaginary landscape*. The mental walk enables people to become immersed in a memory path, to lower their level of consciousness, and thus free their creative imagination through fertile correspondences. The walk inscribes people in this landscape and sets in motion the whole mechanism. The path is split into *sequences* that succeed each other in a precise order, where for memorizing it is no longer enough to place the elements to be remembered in a certain order, whether chronological or logical, but rather to associate an idea to an image placed within a particular order. Each sequence arouses the invention of short *animated scenes*, the images of which will be mentally *projected*, with each new walk, into the stopping places along the itinerary. The arts of memory prefigure indeed the arrival of moving images.

Why awaken the present to this (hi)story? Because the arts of memory appear to be a marker of the way of thinking of each period, like a black box of the representations of the world that humans are capable of inventing. Also because the very movement of history and its changes of paradigm shed new light on the constructions of the arts of memory. The individualized and intimate places (*loci*) of the ancient palaces of memory become collective and porous. The unique and secret images (*imagines*) that nourish these arts become multiple and public. The fixed image shaped by a moving observer is replaced by a moving image received by a fixed observer. The dialectical place-image links become collective intelligence, film sequences, or interactive sites. New technologies enable us to go from constructions of a finite number of possibilities to systems with infinite combinations. These systems renew the notion of the labyrinth, as a mental walk with multiple meanings among symbolic enigmas. The walk itself goes from one waymarked path to many connected paths. The augmented reality of these new virtual landscapes, and the links that can be woven there, are central to artistic investigation and the development of knowledge today.

During a period of obscurantism, which was nevertheless at the frontier of modern times, one man more than any other contributed to transmitting an improbable link between the ancient invention of the arts of memory and the contemporary arts. This man, Giordano Bruno, burned at the stake by the Inquisition in 1600, is the embodiment of *homo nexus* (from the Latin nexus: knot, link, connection), the nexialist who could become contemporary man, as creator of meanings, forms, and connections. Bruno took elements of the Cabal and Neoplatonism to spark off a global revolution in the ways of thinking in the late Renaissance. Inspired by Ramon Llull, and ahead of Copernicus, he placed links, or more precisely the magic of links, at the center of his action. "The Faustian character of Bruno, at the dawn of modernity, seems to me to be the ideal go-between for introducing the contemporary artist to the magic of the link, that is to say, in fact, to a practical wisdom of connection."[3] Bruno placed the striking scenes of the ancient arts of memory, not

[3] Thierry Bardini, *Les liens de Giordano Bruno : magie, arts et sciences à l'heure du nexus*, id.erudit.org/iderudit/45642ac.

*The Thinking Machine*
Back in the sixteenth century, Giordano Bruno fought against the unshakeable boundaries that still separate science and consciousness, and science and imagination. The preeminence of links in his systems anticipates the importance of interactions in the modern development of cybernetics.

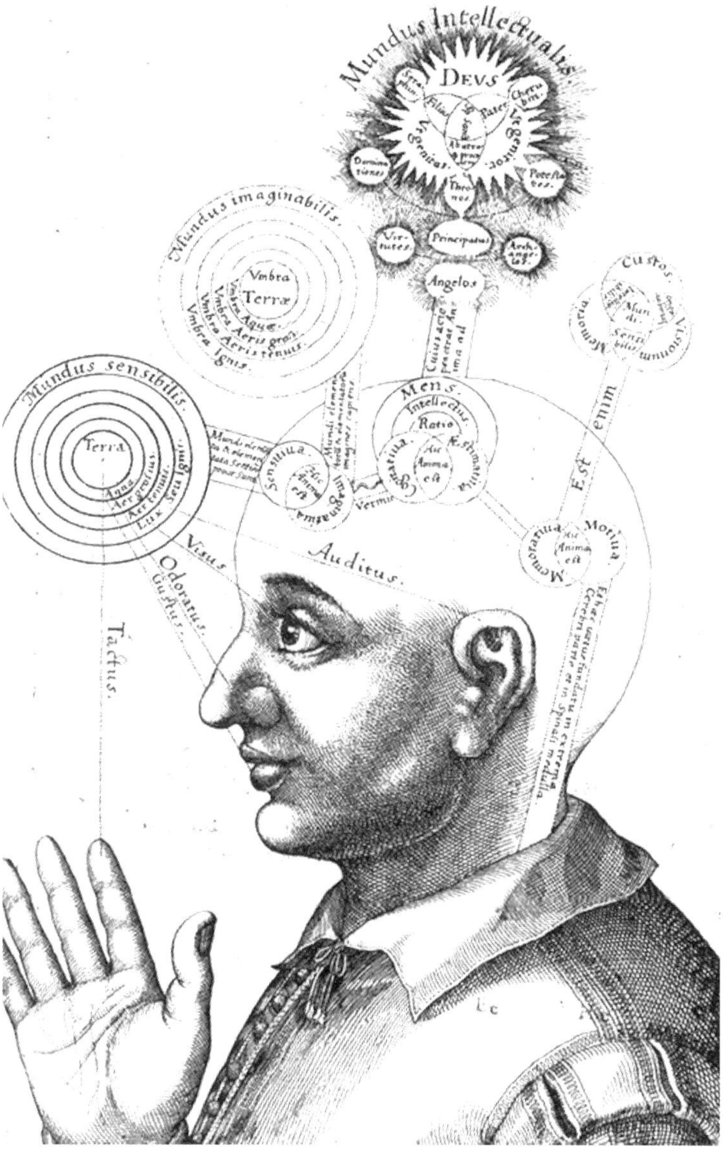


*Man and the Macrocosm,* Robert Fludd, 1574-1637.

in real or imaginary architectures, but on totally dematerialized mechanical structures, sorts of cogwheels driven by complex mechanisms. It could be interpreted as a premonition of cinema three centuries before the fact. Bruno's systems function as heuristic instruments capable of actualizing the infinite number of combinations making up the framework of the real. For him, the link between memory, language, and image is as much a question of science as of magic, because he defines magicians as "wise men, endowed with the capacity to act." From m*agic to image*, Bruno tried to establish a link with the whole, to create a veritable anthropology of the *link.* Today, the ambition of the digital arts may well be to establish this link, which is liable to propel humanity toward a global form of knowledge. It would then be the *place without a place* of a collective experiment never before carried out at such a large scale, that of the infinite expansion of virtual memories and their interactions.

This essay sets out to investigate the situation of the communicating vessels interconnecting the arts of memory and the question of representation today. How has artificial memory, in its successive forms, conserved the dynamic interconnection of ideas, places, and images? What are these places and images, and how do they set themselves in motion in the more general setting in motion of the universe? How does mentally walking enable us to symbolically organize, according to the logic of an itinerary, the images implanted on the medium of a virtual architecture? At the same time as a project is taking shape for a total understanding of the world, we dream of a universal key that will open the representation and transformation of the world. How can the utopia of *a world in the head* take shape when the places and images go from being individual creations to the status of collective representations?

This essay goes from the camera obscura to the cinema, from cabinets of curiosities to virtual landscapes, right up to the digital culture that today gives new life to Mnemosyne's ancient project. This story is formed by a great diversity of experiments over time. I have tried to gather together the different elements, heretofore scattered, and to organize their joint and universal visibility, in accordance with Aby Warburg's idea of *good neighborliness*, in which the solution to a problem was contained not in the book he was looking for but rather in the one next to it in his library.[4] The whole thing could resemble a jigsaw puzzle the pieces of which do not fit together properly, and the limits of which could expand indefinitely. For it is difficult to incorporate the arts of memory in the standard categories of academic knowledge. Yates had already highlighted the problem: we do not know where to categorize studies of this type, even when we know they exist. This essay is therefore a *montage*, in the cinematographic sense of the term. The montage of a film is the orderly sequencing of a series of shots. Each shot may have required several takes. Each take may have changed the scenario. Each cut in the montage may be a new junction in the movie-labyrinth. The elements gathered together here are therefore like rushes on a cutting table, and the final montage is just one among innumerable other possible montages.

[4] The sources of all separate fragments are of course given in notes in the text, and/or in the bibliographical annex. For the rest, for this edifice of masonry built with the thousand-and-one bricks stored in memory over time, and metamorphosed into a new use, I have followed the example of Benjamin. In 1939, in his *Arcade Project*, Benjamin wanted to bring together quotations, materials, interpretations, and theory in a constellation of details for which the reader needed to use imagination, thus closely linking creation and montage: "The theory of the art of quoting without quotation marks is intimately linked to that of montage." Walter Benjamin, *Paris, Capital of the Nineteenth Century – The Arcades Project* (Paris, New York: Belknap Press, 2002).

*Mental Path*

In the ancient palaces of memory, the mental walk activates the memory machine, which activates the image machine. Walking arouses images and generates thought. The walk became physical In the Middle Ages, in prayer paths, then in the gardens in the Renaissance. Walking induces mobility In the gaze, which induces mobility in images. Today, walking in digital virtualities has become an enjoyable, interactive and immersive path, through systems such as the mind map and new knowledge tools.

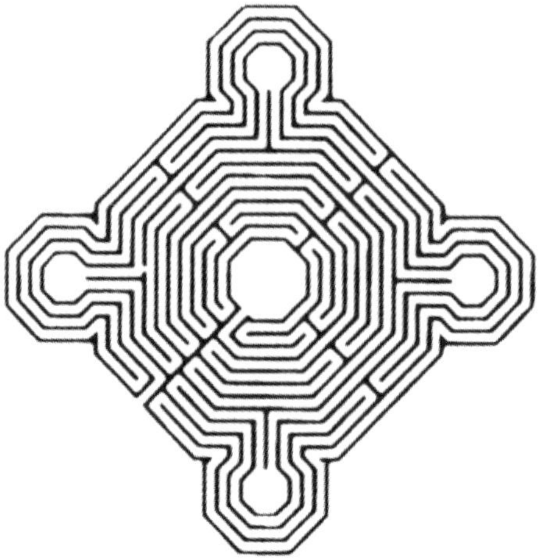

Logotype of a Historical Monument - inspired by the black marble labyrinth inlay in the floor of the nave of the Reims Cathedral, destroyed in 1779.

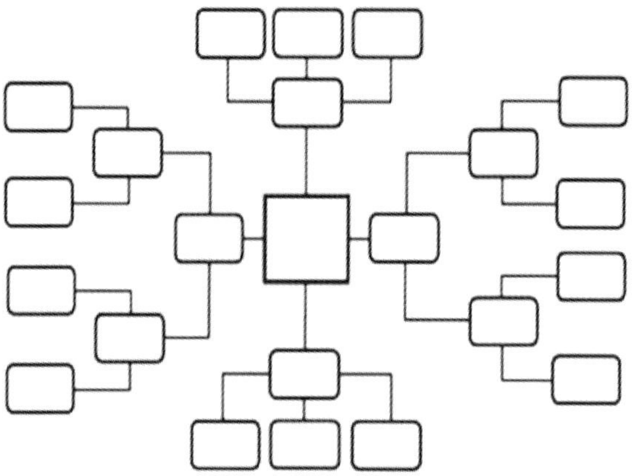

Mind map - concept

# ARTIFICIAL MEMORY

The Greeks did not content themselves with admitting memory into the system of human arts, they also identified its laws and modes of operation, closely related to the world of dreams. In a passage of *On Memory,* Aristotle contemplates the ways in which our mind spontaneously recalls into memory that which escapes it. Everything works, he says, by means of associations: one memory recalls another, the image of one thing leads to another, if there is a relationship of resemblance, contrariety, or contiguity between them. It is therefore possible to use these laws of association as the basis for artificially extending the natural capacities of memory. As Aristotle observes in *On Dreams*, for certain people, the visions that occur during dreams are guided by analogous processes. The art of memory uses these rules to construct its images, which are liable to concentrate in themselves a chain of associations capable of enabling the mind to retrieve the things attributed to them. It is precisely in this constitutive procedure of mnemotechnics that we seize upon a dimension of the art of memory that can be characterized as truly creative. Mnemonic techniques do not just accumulate data, and do not only serve to remember texts that have already been written. They can also contribute to producing texts that can be memorized easily. Fundamentally, we return to the creative powers of Mnemosyne, articulated in a different way.

In the first memory palaces, an idea to be memorized was associated with a striking scene, and the image of that scene implanted in a previously memorized place. This place could be imaginary or inspired by existing architectures. Each stop along an ordered itinerary through this place would therefore summon up an image associated with an idea. This interconnection of *places* (loci) and *images* (imagines) in the first memory palaces required the ability to classify, order, and organize them. It was necessary to be able to rely on an extremely precise and sure memorization of the places. Regarding *order and walking*, the art of memory resembles *montage* in audiovisual creation and the tree structures characteristic of the digital arts. Regarding *loci*, the art of memory anticipates the sense of spatial organization and interaction that would later be at work in the art of gardens and landscaping, architecture and town planning, theater stages, and cabinets of curiosities. Regarding *imagines*, the art of memory prefigures the mental system that would be at work later in animated images and cinema. The more imaginative the image, whether outlandish, fantastic, monstrous, or virtual, the better it is as an aid for memorization. As if its artificial nature, which distinguishes it from the real, were the guarantee of its effectiveness in resisting the erosion that progressively erases every trace. As if thought, too often reduced only to the medium of language, could only be fully deployed by going beyond the war between language and image.

*Art of Loci: the Method of Places*

Simonides of Ceos is said to have been the inventor of artificial memory around 600 BCE. He was an *aoidos*, a wandering lyric poet who hired out his talents to rich patrons. One of them, Scopas of Crannon in Thessaly, asked Simonides to compose an ode in his honor. The evening of the banquet, Simonides devoted half of his ode to eulogizing Castor and Pollux. The angry Scopas only paid him half of the sum agreed and invited him to obtain the other half from the twins. Shortly afterwards, Simonides was called outside because two young people were insistently asking to speak with him. He went out, but found nobody. At the same moment, the room in which Scopas was dining caved in, causing dozens of deaths, and leaving Simonides as the only survivor. Aid arrived, together with the families of the victims, who panicked because the unrecognizable bodies could not be identified. Simonides, remembering the configuration of the room and the places of the diners, was alone able to name the bodies, thus ensuring them an honorable passage to the afterlife. Instructed by this event, he realized that order is what best guides and illuminates memory.

> He inferred that persons desiring to train this faculty must select localities and form mental images of the facts they wish to remember and store those images in the localities, with the result that the arrangement of the localities will preserve the order of the facts, and the images of the facts will designate the facts themselves, and we shall employ the localities and images respectively as a wax writing tablet and the letters written on it. [...]
> It has been sagaciously discerned by Simonides or else discovered by some other person that the most complete

> pictures are formed in our minds of the things that have been conveyed to them and imprinted on them by the senses, but that the keenest of all our senses is the sense of sight, and that consequently perceptions received by the ears or by reflection can be most easily retained in the mind if they are also conveyed to our minds by the mediation of the eyes.[5]

Thought, place, and image: the triad of the arts of memory was established. In Simonides's wake, the Greeks were to invent a true art of memory, of which there remains very few written traces, but which has nevertheless come down to us through the writings of Ancient Greece and Rome. In a period when no technical means existed for mechanically reproducing writing, the use of effective mnemotechnical techniques was absolutely necessary. From Antiquity to the Renaissance, the image was used as an activator for remembering places. Classical rhetoric, the art of creating convincing discourse, descends itself from that older art, which teaches the memory of images and places and the structuring of the mind through images and places. This art of places, or art of loci, was codified in Greece and then in Ancient Rome by Aristotle *(On Memory and Reminiscence),* Cicero *(De Oratore),* Quintilian *(Institutio Oratoria),* and the unknown author of the treatise *Rhetorica ad Herennium*[6] (long attributed to Cicero).

The method is as follows: you determine an itinerary linking a certain number of places, for example the rooms of a vast palace, which you people with striking or strange characters, objects, or scenes that have some relationship with the things to be remembered. The itinerary through this *memory palace* is always the

[5] Cicero, *De Oratore*, www.laits.utexas.edu/memoria/Cicero.html.

[6] *The Rhetorica ad Herennium,* written by an unknown author around 86-82 BCE, is the only conserved treatise on Latin rhetoric covering the arts of memory, the method of which is precisely described by Yates in *The Art of Memory*.

same. You enumerate the stops, which may be the successive rooms of the palace or the different parts of a room. In your long-term memory, you store the places and the immutable order of the walk from stop to stop. This initial learning of a place requires a long preliminary period of personal work. You now have a ready-to-use memory place. In order to memorize a list of things or notions, you associate with each stop in the place an image of the notion to be remembered. Subsequently, when you have to give a speech, plead your defense, or simply refresh your memory, all you have to do is travel through this architecture in your mind. The walk, along the ordered itinerary, automatically recalls the associated images. The sight of the scenes that happen there and the strange beings you encounter resuscitate the memory of the things you placed there, in the order of the itinerary. The force of this iconic association is such that the associated images create a combination capable of remaining in one's mid-term memory for some time.

The *places* (loci) can be totally imaginary, or evocative of real places. In either case, they need to be minutely known to the experimenter. First, an ordered itinerary through the place must be created and memorized. This itinerary must be studied mentally until it is lastingly integrated into deep memory. The order in which this itinerary or path is inscribed in memory dictates where such or such image, associated with such or such thought, will be placed. It is this perfectly memorized order that ensures the effectiveness of the work in the opposite direction, during the mental walk in the memory palace, to revive the images left in each place, and thus the associated thoughts.

The *images* (imagines) are invented by the experimenter each time, in such a way that establishes an indestructible link between the idea to be memorized, the place, and the image. Veritable striking scenes, peopled with eccentric characters, are mentally placed at each stop along the itinerary in the memory palace. To do this, the images created must be active (*imagines agentes*). They will work all the better if they are totally incongruous in the memory place: dazzling, irrational, sexual, scatological; in other words, the most likely to trigger an emotional shock that automatically recalls the idea memorized.

How is it possible to procure these places and images, these fantastic visions to be subsequently incorporated in these architectures? If imagination were lacking, real architectures could be used to inspire the places. As for the images, more or less anything was allowed. In order to remember the elements of a poisoning trial, the anonymous author of *Rhetorica ad Herennium* pictures the victim in bed and the accused by the side of the bed, holding a cup in his right hand, a tablet in his left, and the testicles of a goat. The cup recalls the poisoning, the tablet the inheritance, and the testicles the witnesses (*testes* in Latin). The succession of such images on a path could result in a sort of mental film. The Catholic Church disapproved of the use of magic and various drugs, but it is certain both were used, together with the most obscene images:

> After designing a memory location on conventional lines, he then positioned in each an object – a chamber pot, a box of salve, a bowl of plaster were his first three examples – and then had separate figures, each based on individuals he knew well and each carefully named, jolt the scene into mnemonic action. Thus in rapid sequence Grataroli presented his friend Peter as picking up the chamber pot full of urine and pouring it over James, Martin putting his finger in the ointment box and wiping it over Henry's anus, and Andrew taking some plaster from the bowl

*Congestorium Artificiose Memoriae* by Johannes Romberch (1520)
Diagram of the Places of Memory.

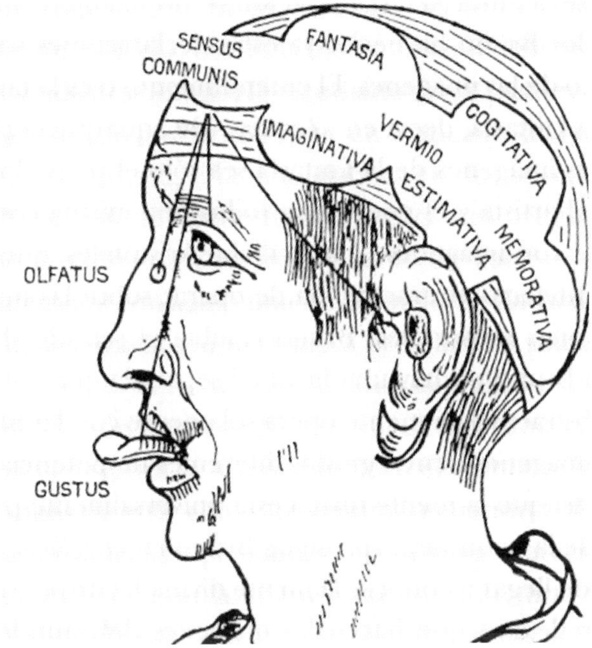


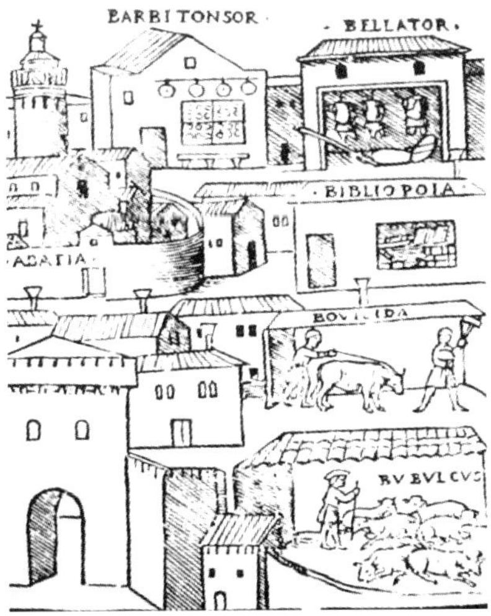


*Congestorium Artificiose Memoriae* by Johannes Romberch (1520).
Mnemonic System.

*Artificial Memory*

"The man who knows by heart how Zora is made, if he is unable to sleep at night, can imagine he is walking along the streets and he remembers the order by which the copper clock follows the barber's striped awning, then the fountain with the nine jets ... This city which cannot be expunged from the mind is like an armature, a honey-comb in whose cells each of us can place the things he wants to remember: names of famous men, virtues, numbers, vegetable and mineral classifications, dates of battles, constellations, parts of speech. Between each idea and each point of the itinerary an affinity or a contrast can be established, serving as an immediate aid to memory."

Italo Calvino. *Invisible Cities*, trans. William Weaver, (Orlando: Harcourt Brace, 1974).

> and smearing it over Francis's face. If one could link these vignettes by pun, analogy, or association of ideas to given concepts, one could be guaranteed never to forget them.[7]

The art of memory is a private art, the images and places are used only by the person practicing it. We therefore have few examples of it. Some of those images, or their components, are more closely related to orality than to written text. They need to be read out loud, as is the case for understanding certain coats of arms. Some are purely and simply plays on words, phonetic approximations, rebuses, like these examples mentioned by Fulcanelli:

> Nothing shocks our modernism more than these tavern signs swinging on an ironwork pole; we recognize the letter O followed by a K with a line through it, but the drunkard of the sixteenth century made no mistake and entered the *grand cabaret* without hesitation.[8] *Hostelries* often displayed a golden lion frozen in a heraldic pose, which, for the wanderer in search of shelter, signified that *one could sleep there*, thanks to the double meaning of the image.[9] (...) Here there is absolutely identical figuration and meaning as the Cabala expressed in the woodcuts of certain works, in particular *The Dream of Polyphili*.[10]

After Cicero, we encounter the art of memory again in Quintilian and Saint Augustin, whose *City of God* can be considered as one of the first examples of imaginary urbanism:

> I come to the fields and spacious memory palaces where are the treasures of innumerable images, brought into it from things of all sorts perceived by the senses. There is stored up,

[7] Jonathan D. Spence, *The Memory Palace of Matteo Ricci*, (New York: Viking-Penguin, 1984).
[8] A play on words in French: "au cabaret" abbreviated to "O K".
[9] Another play on words "au lion d'or" (at the Golden Lion) sounds the same in French as "au lit on dort" (in bed one sleeps).
[10] Fulcanelli, *The Dwellings of the Philosophers*, www.cista.net/Houses/, trans. Brigitte Donvez and Lionel Perrin.

> whatever besides we think, either by enlarging or diminishing, or any other way varying those things which the sense hath come to; and whatever else hath been committed and laid up, which forgetfulness hath not yet swallowed up and buried. When I enter there, I require instantly what I will to be brought forth, and something instantly comes; others must be longer sought after, which are fetched, as it were out of some inner receptacle; others rush out in troops, and while one thing is desired and required, they start forth, as who should say, "Is it perchance I?" These I drive away with the hand of my heart from the face of my remembrance; until what I wish for be unveiled, and appear in sight, out of its secret place. Other things come up readily, in unbroken order, as they are called for; those in front making way for the following.[11]

Until the Middle Ages, the arts of memory were taught alongside rhetoric as an essential device for the oral transmission of knowledge, and as an instrument of meditation. With Ramon Llull (thirteenth century), then Giordano Bruno (fourteenth century), the arts of memory evolved toward veritable conceptual machineries, brought *the world into the head* and developed "as increasingly elaborate representations of the world, to the point of constructing veritable world systems, in imaginary theaters, with as many levels as planets, and innumerable drawers, floors, and skies for classification."[12]

### *Toward the Collective Use of Memory Palaces*

The art of memory returned in the Middle Ages, through Albert the Great and Thomas Aquinas, and manifested itself in books of stone and images—cathedrals. Just as other rhetorical instruments developed by the Pagan world, the art of memory therefore

[11] Saint Augustin, *Confessions*. qtd. in Yates.
[12] Alain Montesse, *Nouvelles technologies et arts de la mémoire*, (Paris: Editions 00h00, 2002). *alain.montesse.free.fr*

persisted in the Christian world, but at a certain price: it was used and reconstituted in the resemblance of Christian doctrine, which Yates calls "the mediaeval transformation of a classical art" (53). Its aim was to incessantly remind the faithful, who generally could not read, of the necessity and means of achieving their salvation. The art of memory was to be found in meditation, an interior process during the course of which the author discovered, sounded out, selected, and rearranged the material that his memory had carefully gathered together, thus inventing a new work. It was under the influence of the great preaching orders of the late Middle Ages that the methods of the ancient arts of memory returned. The Stations of the Cross are the most obvious ones used by the Christians. The faithful inevitably remembered the story of Christ's Passion, divided into fourteen sequences of the ascent to Golgotha. This sacred drama, thanks to its indisputable sequential stability, became the ultimate mnemonic medium. The collective practice of the arts of memory was also to be found in religious processions, which assimilated a district of a town to a mental map in which the relative locations of the religious buildings, consecrated places, and the design of the routes themselves were all markers and mnemonic schemes. Finally, the arts of memory were to be found in the cosmos,

> by organizing the stars in constellations, the aim was not representation (mimesis), but rather to help people, who needed to find the position of various stars, to identify them by means of a recognizable pattern that they could retrieve in their memory immediately and without risk of error. A map of the sky is therefore both *solemnis* and *rarus*[13], to cite the two

[13] In the Middle Ages, *imagines agentes* were moralistic and should be conceived as symbols of spiritual intentions memorized on the basis of an ordered arrangement in a solemn and rare edifice.

qualities dear to Albert the Great. The constellations were thus mnemotechnical tools.[14]

The Christian West was obviously not the only geographical area where this interconnection of thought, places, and images occurred. In different forms around the world, the same idea could be found of an itinerary through iconic representations of knowledge. For Carlo Severi,

> a logic of memorization by the image guides a number of traditions referred to as *oral* until the present time. In both its ancient and medieval forms, the Western case definitively appears as one of the possible forms of an ideal series of thought exercise techniques leading to the establishment of a tradition.[15]

In this anthropology of the arts of memory, the Nazca Lines are indubitably the most fascinating example of the *other* arts of memory. In the south of Peru, 400 km from Lima and 50 km from the coast, in an area of more than 500 $km^2$, a prodigious book of images is spread across the ground, which features straight lines or zigzags, geometric figures of astonishing perfection, and silhouettes of animals. The lines are combined with geometric shapes, generally converging trapezoidal bands, as broad as boulevards, leading nowhere, without any apparent origin or destination—absurd links between two voids. For the Nazca people, for more than a thousand years, the system of lines served as an agricultural calendar. Observation of the movements of the points of the rising and setting of the sun and moon on the horizon enabled them to predict important events, notably the arrival of high waters in the rivers fed by the rains of the Andes. The points of tangency of the heavenly

[14] Régine Detambel, "L'art de la mémoire", *www.detambel.com/f/index.php?sp=liv&livre_id=1168.*
[15] "Anthropologie et histoire des arts de la mémoire", Paris 17 March 2009, *art.rituel.memoire.free.fr.*

bodies on the horizon also determined the ceremonies and feasts that accompanied sowing and harvesting.

The Nazca Lines were also outlines dedicated to certain rites, diagrams for performing sacred dances, and paths of ritual processions. In fact, the figures consist of a single line, which can be walked entirely in a single go, without discontinuity. The outline created *without lifting the pencil* was propitious for a ritual of declamation, which was cadenced by walking. The Nazca Lines constitute an open-air memory palace, similar to the Greek memory palaces, and at about the same period, combining places, images, and abstract thought, with their interconnection activated by walking. The Western example should not be considered as a universal model, but as one of the forms of social memory practices and iconic representations. Any memory technique is also a technique of the imagination. In that sense, the Nazca Lines even have the form of an art of memory, which implies a combination of two orders of phenomena. On the one hand, the mnesic trace, the classification and chains of inferences that it involves; and on the other hand, the process of evocation, conceptualization, and poetic imagination.

In India, Buddhist monks use mandalas as an aid to meditation. In Sanskrit, mandala means circle. Whereas the uninitiated person sees only geometric shapes or a gathering of divinities, the experienced user will attribute a precise meaning to each figure. The composition as a whole also has a precise meaning. In the long spiritual journey toward *awakening*, the person meditating mentally travels the different parts of the mandala, which are like the rooms in a memory palace. At the center there is the principal divinity, who represents the essence of things, the supreme goal of this meditation. Around the central divinity, there is a concentric zone where a whole court of deities is represented. The doors, pillars, walls, and colors all have symbolic meaning. Each mandala is a figurative representation of the celestial world, and a doorway into that world.

In the Christian West, the art of memory moved from the domain of rhetoric to that of ethics. Christianization transformed a technique, used by the orator to recall what he wanted to remember, into a didactic method intended to imprint in Christians's souls what they must not forget.

> The art of memory thus changed from a personal, private, imaginary, and immaterial art into a monumental, official, public art for the benefit of an institution. It was no longer just a question of memorizing the different elements regarding such or such particular affair, but of representing the whole world, on earth, above and below it, now, before, and after.[16]

The supposed predilection of the Middle Ages for the grotesque and bizarre in painting, statuary, and Illumination could therefore be simply an effect of the mnemonists, who recommended using striking images. The design of the memory palace was no longer only the secret recipe of the orator, it also concerned the very representation and communication of the speech. All the conditions were satisfied for mnemonic systems of places and images to have a public existence; in other words, to be described, painted, sculpted, and finally constructed and used collectively.

### *Combinatorial Art and Dynamic Representation*

Far from reciting by heart, the aim of the art of memory was to serve the composition and encourage the elaboration of new thoughts. Albert the Great had understood that mnemonic places were purely pragmatic. They could induce resemblances with

[16] Alain Montesse, "Arts de la mémoire en ligne", colloquium Image et Mémoire, GrIMH Lyon 21-23 Nov. 2002, *alain.montesse.voila.net.*

existing things, but had no reality in themselves. It would be best to consider them as notional processes that the mind itself produced in order to activate memory. Already for Plato, true knowledge consisted in recalling the ideas that the soul had seen. In that respect he is the father of the renascent art of memory, which was no longer concerned about persuasion, but truth. The Middle Ages, on the contrary, followed the Aristotelian tradition of the image, imbued with a moral sense so as to impact the mind religiously. When Saint Thomas practiced the art of memory, it was to help the faithful reach Heaven and preserve them from Hell. The image was sacred; it indicated a direction to follow and defined good and evil. Dante's *Divine Comedy*, for example, can be seen as a system of representations intended to memorize heaven and its delights, or hell and its torments, by means of striking images distributed in an ordered series of places. The scholar of the Middle Ages thus transmitted from generation to generation the techniques for classifying the elements of thought and the taste for the use of allegory:

> the art of memory could translate words into images and images into words; it contributed to creating written texts, speeches given in public, painted, illuminated and sculpted images, and products that combined words and images such as the *Bilderbücher;* it oriented in particular the reciprocal play of reflection between the words read or heard, the images seen and the images constructed in the mind, which are objects of meditation and contemplation.[17]

Around 1280, at the same time as the classical, scholarly, iconic architectural art of memory was flowering on the European continent, the Majorcan Ramon Llull, in contact with the Jews of the

[17] Lina Bolzoni, "The Play of Images: the Art of Memory from Its Origins to the Seicento", *The Enchanted Loom: Chapters in the History of Neuroscience*, (Oxford: Oxford UP, 1991)--our trans. from the French.

Mediterranean, devised another that was totally different, independent, and based on a very personal interpretation of the Cabala. In his *Ars Brevis,* Ramon Llull broke with all the figurative construction of the ancient memory palace to create pure mental speculations by means of algebraic and combinatorial formulae. This divinatory practice aimed to reveal that which was absent or in the making, or unknown, by establishing coincidences of places and calculations of correspondences. It involved manipulating mobile wheels or disks to study certain combinations, and to form by permutation the secret names of the spiritual powers.

Llull and his *Combinatorial Art* represent a transition point for a tradition that crossed the whole scholastic period and medieval Platonism. At first sight, the Art of Ramon Llull appears to be a form of logic: it proposed to resolve problems and answer questions by manipulating letters on geometrical figures. However, Ramon Llull claimed that his *Ars Magna* (the title of one of his major works) was much more than logic: it was a method for achieving knowledge through the power of symbolic representations. It was no longer a matter of objects, or figurative images, distributed in architectural settings, but rather a combinatorial system of abstract alphanumeric signs engraved on cogwheels. Set in motion, this machinery engendered the combinatorial meeting of the letters, and therefore the re-composition of things, and even the re-creation of the world. It was almost a sort of algebraic-metaphysical calculation. More importantly, and a new development, it went from a static system to a dynamic representation. It was no longer a question of decor or architecture, in which humans traced their paths, but the more or less autonomous movement of machinery, of a machination:

> Ramon Llull introduces movement into memory. The figures of his Art, on which its concepts are set out in the letter notation,

*Combinatorial Art*

Ramon Llull introduced movement into images and abstraction into mental speculation. The interplay of non-figurative combinations is a means of attaining knowledge through the power of symbolic systems. This transition toward a pure combinatorial system was a key moment in the mechanization of knowledge.

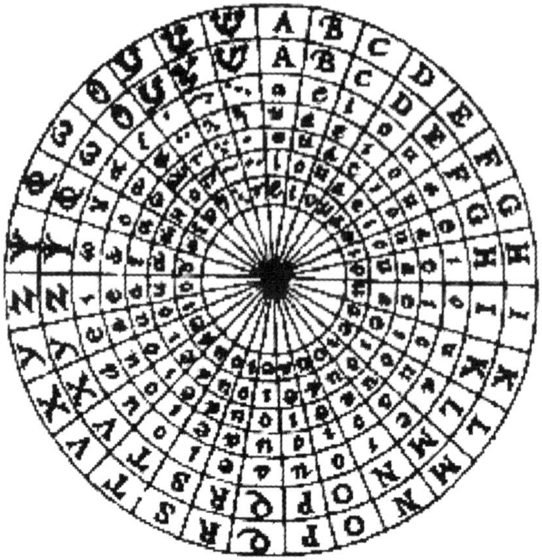

Memory wheels, *De Umbris Idearum,* Giordano Bruno, 1582.

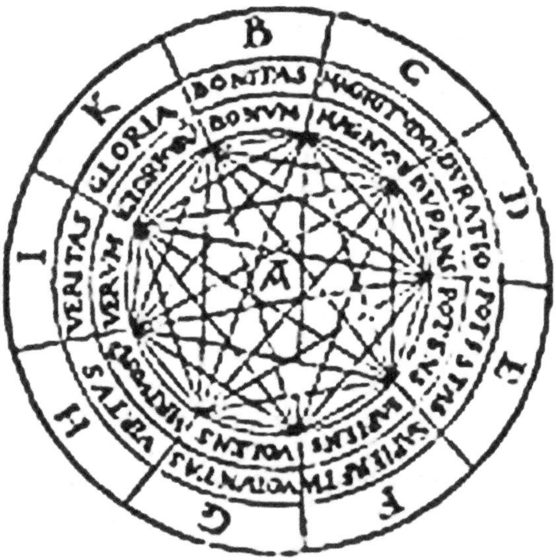


*Ars Brevis,* Ramon Llull, Pisa, 1308.

are not static but revolving. One of the figures consists of concentric circles, marked with the letter notations standing for the concepts, and when these wheels revolve, combinations of the concepts are obtained. In another revolving figure, triangles within a circle pick up related concepts. These are simple devices, but revolutionary in their attempt to represent movement in the psyche.[18]

Llull's *Ars Magna* was broadly disseminated and quickly spread throughout Europe, as far as Germany, where it attracted the interest of Nicholas of Kues. After the fall of Constantinople (1453), it was taken up and developed by Giovanni Pico della Mirandola and other authors, who almost completely identified Lullism with the Cabala (although Llull himself did not explicitly use Hebrew letters). During the Renaissance, the *Ars Magna* nourished the Neoplatonic magic that was developing in Italy and throughout Europe. In addition to Robert Fludd (*Ars Memoriæ*), Ficino, Tommaso Campanella (*The City of the Sun),* and Pico della Mirandola, two figures stand out in particular—Giulio Camillo and Giordano Bruno.

Camillo (1480–1544) imagined a *Theater of Memory*, in Italy and then France, where he offered a wooden model of it to Francis I. The aim of this theater is more magical than pragmatic, but it is constructed like a real theater, with images that guide and support thought, and, rather than enabling a full understanding of the orator's discourse, lead to wisdom. The edifice, in the form of an amphitheater with seven sections, was intended as an *imago mundi*, where all ideas and objects can find an appropriate place due to the planetary series to which they belong. The series were formed on the basis of correspondences established between a particular planet and certain animals, plants, and minerals. For example, the

[18] Yates 176.

lion, gold, and the heliotrope belong to the Sun series. The matter symbolized by the figures of the theater also came from Florentine Platonism. The aim was to construct a cosmic figure by which the spectator hoped to obtain benefits from the universe. The position of the solitary spectator was not where the audience would normally be, but on stage, whence he could contemplate the theater as a vision of the universe. Giulio Camillo called this edifice "a *constructed soul*, because one can physically see what the mind conceives, but the eye cannot perceive at all." It was also about putting in order, classifying the diversity of things and events, through the invention of appropriate places and images that enabled the spectator to master the chaos of the world and things. These theaters of the world were perhaps the last encyclopedic places, which condense and classify knowledge, designed in function of the art of memory. The Theater of Memory was a vision of the world.

Combinatorial art cannot therefore be reduced simply to the formal logic that governs the new technologies, or the characteristics of a contemporary cognitive economy. It also refers to the very logic by which our memories, lives, and minds operate, about which the ancient arts of memory first had the brilliant intuition. Pierre Lévy argues very astutely that, just as much as the usefulness of searching for information, it is the vertiginous sensation of diving into the collective brain and participating in it that explains the Internet craze. Meanwhile, in the foreword to Camillo's *The Theater of Memory*, Bertrand Schefer notes that:

> It is easy to see in it all sorts of anticipations concerning the evolution and classification of the means of communication we use today, a theoretical guarantee for some modern sciences or virtual realities, by observing the following: the

Diagram of the cosmos in the form of a horoscope, Giordano Bruno, 1582.

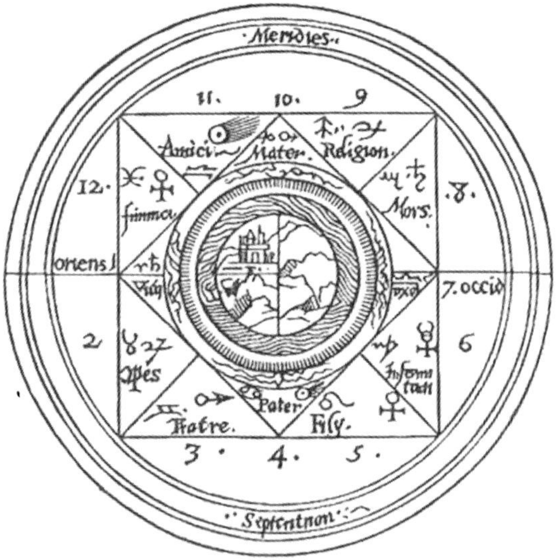


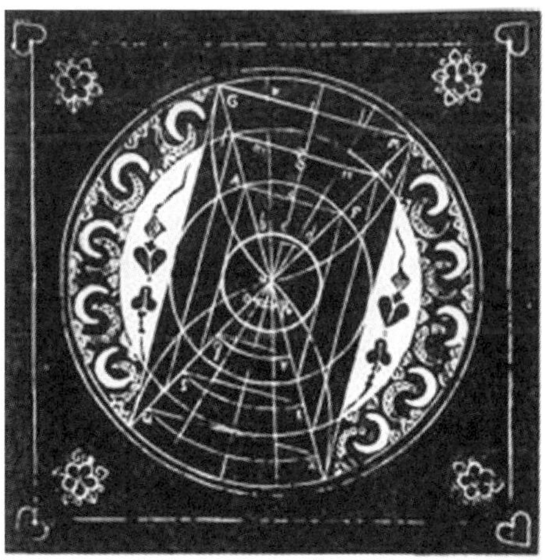

Figure by Giordano Bruno – *Articuli Adversus Mathematicos,* Prague, 1588.

*L'homo-nexus*

Homo nexus, the man whose reason for being is the bond according to Giordano Bruno, prefigures a time maybe in the near future, when bioinformatic inventions might reconcile life and matter, organization and creation, poetry and technoscience. The arts of memory would thereby be more connected to nexialism, the name of a metascience invented by the science fiction writer A. E. van Vogt. The nexialist seeks to produce non-compartmentalized science, which is not simply the aggregate of all the separate sciences, but goes beyond them through a permanent interconnection.

> Theater of Memory was erected on new bases that now constitute the foundations of the practice and vocabulary of the new encyclopedia: sites, icons, windows, portals, links, and hypertexts.[19]

*Magic Art and the Expansion of the Universe*

In the sixteenth century, Bruno already intended to memorize the entire universe by means of a series of correspondences and associations unified by the celestial system. He thus brought the arts of memory to their apotheosis. The three currents of Hermeticism, Mnemonics, and Lullism were closely interwoven in the complex personality and mission of Bruno, who was passionate about the art of Ramon Llull and wrote several works in Latin on the subject, including *The Lamp of Combinations according to Lull* and *Progress and the Hunter's Lamp of Logical Methods*.

> While the old Aristotelian physics were caught up in a fatal crisis, the alchemical and magical doctrines appeared; in other words, the techniques aimed at transforming things, the experimental arts which, in their impiety, were intended to transgress the laws of nature and overturn the physical order, throw the stars out of orbit, transform the living and resuscitate the dead.[20]

Bruno attempted a bold synthesis of the classical art of memory and Lullian art by animating the combinatorial of images. He imagined the idea of replacing the letters on the cogwheels of Ramon Llull's machineries by the striking scenes and strange beings of the

[19] Giulio Camillo, *Le Théâtre de la Mémoire,* (trans. from Italian by Eva Cantavenera and Bertrand Schefer, (prefaced by *Les lieux de l'image* by Bertrand Schefer), Paris: Ed. Allia, 2001 (our trans. from the French trans.).
[20] Eugenio Garin, *Moyen Âge et Renaissance*, (Paris: Gallimard, 1969).

bygone memory palaces. "The innermost circle or wheel of the star images — the central power station of the magically animated memory."[21] Montesse makes an audacious suggestion concerning the cogwheels on which the moving images are inscribed: Was not cinema invented three centuries ago by Giordano Bruno?[22]

Bruno's systems proved to be much more complex than mere mnemotechnical artifices. Their value is above all as a model of ideal knowledge, a heuristic instrument capable of actualizing the infinite relations and combinations that make up the fabric of the real. For Bruno, as had already been the case for Camillo, constructing and working with images were not ordinary operations or an arbitrary act linked only to subjective criteria of efficacy. On the contrary, it meant taking possession of the *shadows*, the *seals* that ideas had left in the world, and re-following the traces of shadows projected onto the plurality of visible things.

Bruno's *hero* is an accomplished manipulator of phantasms and images. In his *frenzies* and trances, he attains a sort of second state, the supreme form of ecstasy, in which the *imaginatum caelum* (the intelligible world as it is imagined by the operator during his practice of manipulating the phantasms) corresponds to transcendental reality. Bruno tried to attain a kind of operative magic, an operational mastery of *phantasms*. *De Vinculis in Genere*, deals with bonding, seizing, and winning the loyalty of those that onc wants to influence. Couliano recognizes in *De Vinculis* the direct ancestor of the modern discipline of applied psychosociology.[23]

Couliano also recognizes the existence of two very distinct grammars, that of spoken language and that of fantastic language.

[21] Yates 217.
[22] Cinémaginaire 3, (May 1993).
[23] Ioan Peter Couliano, *Eros and Magic in the Renaissance*, Paris, trans. Margaret Cook, (Chicago: U of Chicago P. 1987).

Only the intellect has the privilege of understanding the fantastic grammar. The body opens a window on the world for the soul via the five organs of the senses, through which the messages arrive before being codified and transformed into *phantasms* directly perceptible by the soul. The soul has primacy over the body. Bruno along with all the members of the Neoplatonic current during the Renaissance attributed great power to phantasms, and to learning how to manipulate and transmit them. The phantasm thus held absolute primacy over the spoken word, preceding both the articulation and the comprehension of all linguistic messages. The investigations initiated by Bruno with the manipulation of phantasms therefore concerned first of all the status of images. The *anima mundi* is replaced by the *imago mundi*, which draws a double representational path: an exterior path toward the vast outside world, and an interior path directly linked to the conscious corporeity that Cesarano would theorize in the twentieth century.[24]

In *De Umbris Idearum*, Bruno proposes an occult version of the Lullian art of memory, and uses magical imagery to arrange the stars and all their attributes on Llull's combinatorial cogwheels. His system is the exact opposite of the method used by Llull, who had carefully avoided images. His new mnemotechnical system was based on concentric wheels with thirty compartments, corresponding to the twenty-three letters of the Latin alphabet, four Greek characters, and three Hebrew characters. Bruno attributed to these letters a symbolism derived from Egyptian hieroglyphs "which took, to designate particular objects, figures derived from nature or from parts of things."[25] This system was inspired by Ramon Llull's *Ars brevis*, and by the combinatorial system of the Cabala. It could

[24] Giorgio Cesarano, *Manuale di sopravivvenza*, (Bari: Dedalo, 1974).
[25] Giordano Bruno, *De Magia*, c. 1590 (our trans. from the French).

produce the memory images corresponding to all words, by associating the mnemonic figures to their different syllables. The potential combinations of these wheels could engender an infinite number of words and their imaginary representations.

In *De Magia* – date unknown, Bruno drifts through the labyrinth of mnemotechnical constructions, probably inspired by reading Heinrich Cornelius Agrippa. "There is no latent or separate force in the or on Earth that the magician cannot revive or unite",[26] wrote Giovanni Pico della Mirandola. Magic should obviously not be interpreted as fertility rites or incantations to make the rain fall. It was rather the incarnation of a very old desire: "To touch with thought and think with the body. To open doors. To get back to unity. In short, to assimilate the ancient and still living conception of the universe as a loving order of correspondences and not as a blind chain of causes and effects."[27] *De Magia* resembles a memory palace where one walks from room to room in one's imagination to recall the steps in a thought process, and it is a palace of delirious proportions and ramifications: the nine categories of magic, its three principal species corresponding to the degrees of reality of the world, the two species of efficient force, the double movement that animates each thing, the twenty types of bonds... The arts and sciences are arranged, or rather thrown together pell-mell, without apparent order, in series of rooms, atria, and divisions of manic complexity.

What does Bruno give us a glimpse of in his composition uniting all these images behind this iconography of the Renaissance? He gives the impression of inversing the trend of the

[26] Giovanni Pico della Mirandola, *900 Philosophical, Cabalistic and Theological Conclusions*, in Stephen A. Farmer, *Syncretism in the West: Pico's 900 Theses*, (Tempe Arizona: MRTS, 1998)-our adaptation.
[27] Octavio Paz in André Breton, *L'Art magique - une histoire de l'art*, (Paris: Phébus, 1991).

early Renaissance, whereby the more archaic images evolved toward a classical form. He dramatized the doctrine of *anima mundi*, affirming that the world lives, breathes, and even thinks. He combined the thinking of Lucretius, Nicolas of Kues (for whom the universe was *interminable*, neither finite nor infinite), and Copernicus, contradicted Aristotle, put the sun at the center of our universe, and attained that astonishing vision of an infinite extension of the universe. For Bruno, the universe was unlimited and all is motion. These revolutionary ideas were seen as dangerous. On February 17, 1600, Bruno was burned at the stake by the Inquisition, brought before it because of his freedom of mind, refusal to accept dogma, Copernican intuition, and vision of the infinite nature of the world. Since he declared that he "had no desire to repent, had no reason to repent, and had nothing to repent for," it was consequently decided to burn both his books and their author.

***Mental walking*** is the method that set the memory palaces in motion. Walking designates the movement of a person along an itinerary that had been so often repeated and memorized that it could be followed nearly automatically, without paying particular attention to it. This lowering of attention enabled the brain to be freed up for other mental activities, little related to immediate necessity. The driving force behind this walking was the dream. Humans dream the world before they actually discover it. Each epoch dreams not only of the next, it also endeavors to become more conscious. We dream of systems that can reproduce the deep rhythm of reality, which go completely beyond the limits of language and image to provide a *clavis universalis*, capable of setting the world in motion. The *dream* is the marker of these systems, at work in the arts of memory, and today in cinema and the contemporary arts. As in dreams, these systems have neither hierarchy of time (no past, present, or future) nor hierarchy of space (distances are abolished in the series of places). As in dreams, life and death live together and are no longer incompatible. As in dreams, no taboo can prevent the use of a particular representation. Mental walking enables us to pass freely from reality to dream, and place to image.

The Greeks invented at least two different words to conceptualize the idea of place. There was *topos* (which would lead to *locus– loci* In Latin) and also *khôra* (which would be closer to the Latin *spatium*). The topos is the place in the geographical sense, as in a map; it is linked to objects and the coordinates that can be used to define it. The khôra is relational; it reveals a bond with a place, not an identity. The places used in the arts of memory are similar to both the topos and the khôra. In Ancient Greece, the memory palace was a very personal and hidden private place. It could be purely imaginary, and resemble the khôra. In the Middle Ages, the memory palace could be highly concrete and appertain to a public building; the art of loci moved into the public arena, in cathedrals and elsewhere. This notion of place was central to the arts of memory and the teaching of rhetoric, and gave rise to *commonplaces*; that is, places known by everyone, which could be used to remind the largest possible number of people of an idea to be shared.

Over time, the notion of place evolved toward more abstraction as did, more generally, the forms of the thought-place-image triad. Such is true of all human inventions. The natural places of the first memory palaces gradually gave way to invented places, propitious to mental wandering, and which set the wanderer's gaze in motion. Mobility was transferred from the gazer to the gaze itself. The gaze became mobile during the walk and learned to vary over time and to change the angles of vision. Walking contributed to the metamorphosis of the artwork by the gazer, and was the method by which the reading of the memory palace determined a *point of view*. The mental walk was a movie camera traveling around the garden of memory. The walk inscribed humans in the landscape, and also the landscape in humans. The landscape of the world organizes our mental landscape. The traveler, walker, and rambler make the landscape become readable, like a text, and this reading in turn modifies their perception of the world, and its evocation.

### *The Mental Walk: A Vector of Metamorphosis*

From the medieval *hortus conclusus*[28] to the creations of the Baroque epoch, numerous examples of parks and gardens can be cited with symbolic, emblematic, and figurative mechanisms that resemble those of mnemonic image systems. In many cases, their scenographic arrangements even appertain directly to memory palaces, as in Boboli, the Villa Lante, or the Villa d'Este. This close relationship between memory palaces and the art of gardens is attested to by the large number of spiritual sources they have in common. From Democritus to Petrarch or Franceso Colonna in his *Dream of Poliphilus*, it is striking to see how these authors distinguish themselves in one and the other, thus revealing through their example the profound affinity linking the act of cultivating one's memory to that of tending one's garden.

We shall never know whether Bruno knew the Gardens of Bomarzo in Tuscany. Yet a real walk in this garden reveals the alchemy Bruno sought, the dynamic association of places and striking images likely to *set in motion* the most complex thoughts. Not far from Viterbe, the so-called Park of the Monsters is a Renaissance garden commissioned by Vincino Orsini, Duke of Bomarzo (1528 –1588). A highly cultivated humanist, he created the garden on the death of his wife Giulia Farnese. He did not call it *jardino* but rather *sacro bosco*, sacred grove, or *bosco dei monstri*, grove of the monsters. *Monster* should be understood in the sense of the Latin *monstrare*, that which shows and demonstrates, that which clarifies concepts. These monsters are indeed worth seeing, and being shown to the public. To construct this garden, he called upon the services of one of the greatest gardeners and architects

[28] In the *Song of Songs, the hortus conclusus* (enclosed garden) is identified with the Virgin Mary and appears as a vision of Paradise. In the monastic movement of the Middle Ages, it became a place for the evocation of memory.

of his time, Pirro Ligorio. All the princes of Italy came to visit it, together with innumerable foreign visitors, before it sank into oblivion for many years, until it was rediscovered in the 1950s, when it was the subject of a magnificent book with texts by André Pieyre de Mandiargues and photographs by Georges Glasberg.[29]

It is a garden populated with giant sculptures carved in the bedrock that evoke, by distorting them, most of the myths, principles, and legends that held sway in Antiquity, and were taken up again in the Renaissance. These sculptures are unusual in proportion and bizarre in shape in order to astonish visitors better and oblige them to consider the abstractions they express. From passage to passage and step to step, each element makes up an immense, very Neoplatonist poem to lost love in honor of Orsini's wife. To achieve this, he had to find and then re-create the symbols of a progression that would end with the spouses meeting again, after death. But above and beyond Orsini's own quest, this fantastic garden is a testimony to true love, love that is stronger than death. This search to go beyond death is the incarnation of human desire to take hold of the world in all its diversity. One strolls through the Gardens of Bomarzo from site to site, following a completely ordered itinerary. It is a rite of passage, which resonates with the twists and turns of a true inner journey, punctuated with hopes, trials, discoveries, and metamorphoses. Each site contains one or more inscriptions in Late Latin that invite the visitors to lose themselves, so as to better find themselves. It is a sort of user's guide to the infinity of humanity and its inventions, in a finite and limited space. Another memory palace.

The Gardens of Bomarzo are guarded by two female sphinxes bearing riddles. The walker must reply in order to go forward while

[29] André Pieyre de Mandiargues, *Les Monstres de Bomarzo*, (Paris: Grasset, 1957).

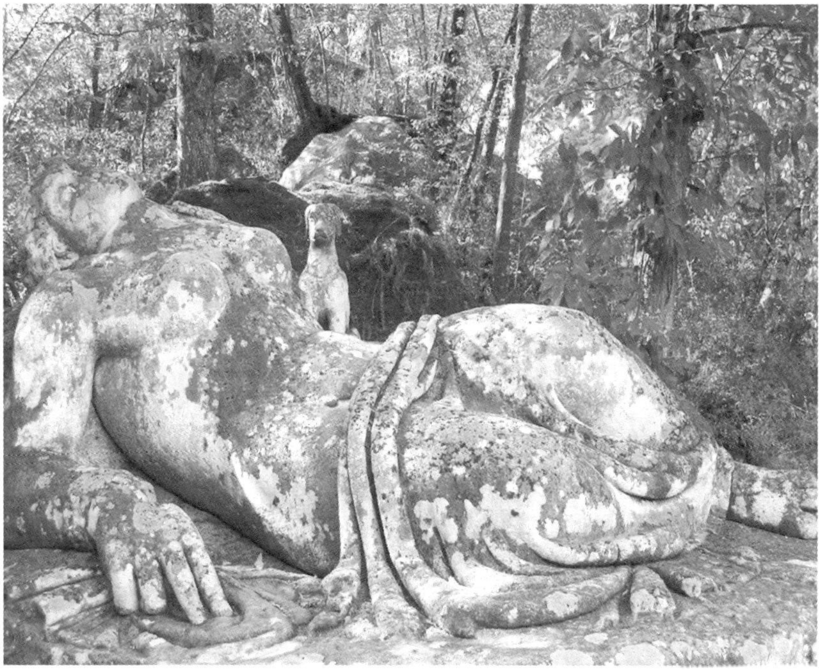

*Sleeping Ariadne and the Mouth of Truth*, Bomarzo Gardens, Tuscany (photos FB).

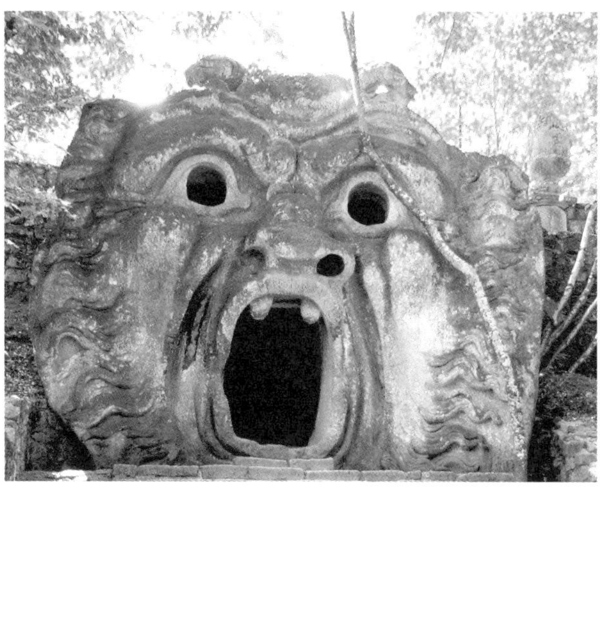

*Bomarzo – the Garden of Memory*

Art, memory, and poetry owe their greatest successes to the collision of disparate terms, the unexpected, the sidestep, the sudden intrusion of something different and sublime. In the order of this disorder, with the help of the forces of nature, a few places have been created by the human hands that relate to the notion of the Great Art, Ars Magna, elucidated by Ramon Llull. None of them correspond better to this attribute than the Gardens of Bomarzo.

meditating on the warning: "Oh you, who enter here, consider what you are seeing and tell me whether so many marvels are conceived as a Lure or as Art." By Art, we should understand the *Ars Magna* of Ramon Llull and the alchemists. Once past the first trials, the walker in Bomarzo plunges into a labyrinth of box hedges. Almost buried by the trees, there is a nine-meter-tall giant. In Ancient Greece, the colossus was not an allusion to size. It designated a man made of stone placed deep in a tomb to replace the absent body of a man who had died without the possibility of recovering his corpse or performing funerary rites. The colossus was not an image: it was a double, as the dead man himself is a double of the living man. A double is not an image at all. It is neither a natural object, nor a mental object, neither an imitation of a real object, nor an illusion of the mind or a creation of thought.

The next discovery is another gigantic statue, a sleeping woman, whose head rests on a stone - arms lay loosely along her sides - and whose torso almost grows from the mountainside. Ariadne is there to say: "You who have passed the trials, you are now entering the realm of dreams." As in mythology, Ariadne offers a thread that will enable the walker to get out of the labyrinth. In a dream, the link between the visible and the invisible world becomes apparent. Thanks to Ariadne's thread, the walker can leave the realm of dreams, the original man is embodied and returns to the Garden of Eden. Henceforth, the walker can apprehend the three worlds - subterranean, terrestrial, and spiritual - which are now as one in the vision of the new man. These three worlds appear grouped together, and are discovered successively in a sort of vertical tracking shot. The subterranean world, the one of the black light of the abyss, is represented by a huge infernal mouth. The white light of the constellations takes on the form of an astrolabe above the mouth.

The *invisible light* is above all the rest, in a fortified town symbolizing the City of God, the heavenly Jerusalem.

One could imagine that it is the immobility of the architectural structure that enables images to be fixed in memory palaces, thus ensuring them greater mnemotechnic permanence. But the rite of passage in the Gardens of Bomarzo reveals exactly the opposite. In fact, the capability of retrieving the images arranged in the memory palace depends on regularly carrying out a journey, a voyage, a *mental walk* in this imaginary architecture. The thing that is memorized, before anything else, is the order of an itinerary oriented by the topology of the architecture. The walker therefore moves not only from one room to another in a memory palace, but also from one memory palace to another.

*Rambling, Dreaming, and Tracking*

To go from reality to dreams, there is only the narrowing of the frame and the choice of the device through which we look, such as the window of a train or bus. The train and the bus are no longer means of transport, but rather a new dwelling, at whose door the merry-go-round of the world places new scenery every day. Uniform commuting and regular movements lead to reverie, the arrangement of memories, and the formulation of new strategies. During the course of a ride, we reorganize our thoughts and remake the world. The mental walk derives from this twofold articulation of creation and traveling, sometimes creating, sometimes traveling, so as to create in return and enable others to travel: this mental walk can also be called *tracking*. The journey is a mobile memory palace, in which the real landscape arouses unpredictable thoughts. The memory palace is an immobile journey, during which constructed

*Uraltes Chymisches Werck,* Abraham Eleazar, 1735.

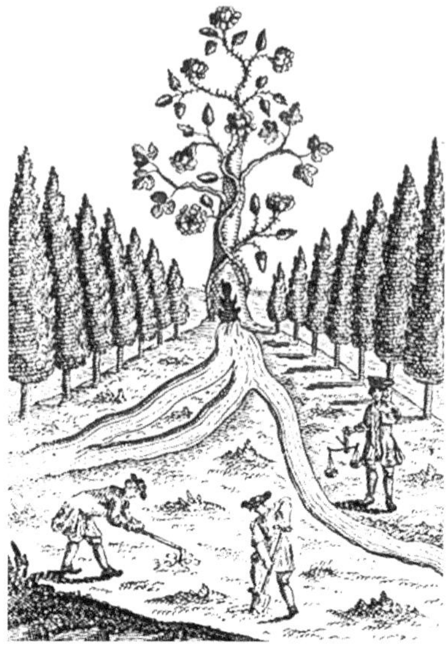

*Birth of a Cosmogony*

We weave symbolic links between our piece of countryside and the cosmos. Starting from where we exist, which is always at the center of the world, in the face of disorder, we organize the cardinal orientation, the natural rhythm (days, seasons, animal migrations …), and the network of meanings that govern them.
The surveying and measuring of space radiate from the center around which the universe gravitates, and define a geometric image of the world and city.

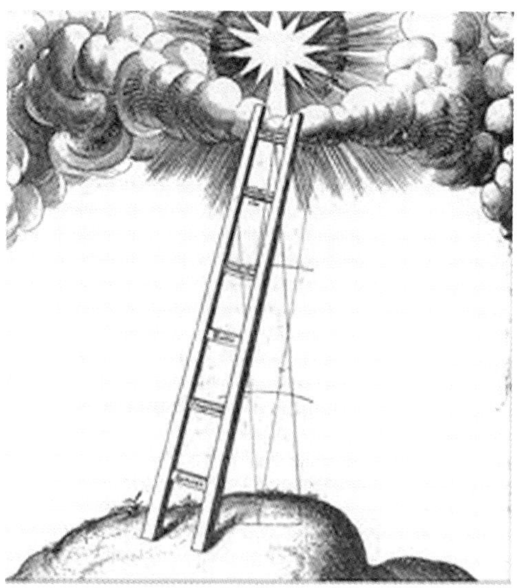

*Jacob's Ladder,* Robert Fludd (1574 – 1637).

thoughts are placed in an improbable landscape. Text and images are in competition, and then become complicit in evoking these theretofore unknown territories. Between drawing and writing, between the graphic design of a map and the linearity of language, a reciprocal relationship is woven: the map becomes a story and the story produces the map. For Gombrich, the image always has the double facets of mirror and map. By map he means the various mental patterns aimed at making representations clearer by simplifying them. The map lends itself to all the games of the imagination. The map is linked to rambling. With his body, man takes the measure of landmarks and distances. In *The Five Senses,* Serres writes about the Gascon countryside:

> the farmer, for thousands of years, has been slowly composing it for the painter, who reveals it to the philosopher in museums and books. He has composed it *pagus* by *pagus*. Now, this same Latin word, from the old agrarian language (as is the verb *pango),* dictates or gives us the "page" — the one that I am plowing in regular furrows this morning with the plowshare of style[30]

In the ancient arts of memory, the incitation to walk is not an invitation to wander, but to explore methodically, in the order of an itinerary. The *Ad Herennium already* recommended perfect visual precision in the representation of the places visited. They

> ought to be neither too bright nor too dim, so that the shadows may not obscure the images nor the lustre make them glitter. I believe that the intervals between backgrounds should be of moderate extent, approximately thirty feet; for, like the external eye, so the inner eye of thought is less powerful when you have moved the object of sight too near or too far away.[31]

[30] *The Five Senses*, (our adaptation of trans. by Margaret Sankey and Peter Cowley (New York: Bloomsbury Academic, 2016).
[31] Anonymous, *Rhetorica ad Herennium* (English trans. by Harry Caplan, Loeb, 1954).

Perspective, which during the Renaissance would regulate the visual exchanges in pictorial art, had not yet taken up its place in this meta-perspective in which spectators are active. It was they who turned their head to perceive what was around them, it was they who chose or changed their points of view. Whether the memory palace was a building, a garden, or a landscape, whether the path was real or imaginary, the vision was formed and reformed every time visitors positioned themselves in a different place. Walkers in the Gardens of Bomarzo experience a certain form of spatiotemporal elasticity, in which all that is required to set the vision in motion is to change the direction of their gaze or the place where they are positioned. Each place, each group of sculptures, each detour to arrive there, was deliberately designed to excite this free play of consciousness and imagination. Anamorphic processes applied not only to painting but also to gardens, the plants and decoration of which were organized in such a way as to lead to the dissipation of forms and the deformation of vision. The effects of dissymmetry and the distortion of perspective change the course of the path and the gaze, decenter the path from the gaze. Drawing his inspiration from "Dürer's window," Athanasius Kircher went so far as to invent his mesoptic instrument (1648) consisting of a frame on a stand, over which was stretched a transparent veil: vision could thus be transformed by the light filtered through the screen, and also by the shadows of silhouettes of people or animals manipulated behind it.

For Marot:

> The garden appears as a medium for giving meaning to landscapes, an art which, by proposing a local syntax for it, enables the diversity of nature to gain access to the status of landscape, ordered in places. The garden was long considered as the place where the geography of the soul met

the geography of nature, and the art of gardens as the conscious undertaking of that meeting. It therefore follows that the garden was undoubtedly not only a special domain in which mnemonic systems could be developed, but also a major setting in which the progressively demolished art of memory could seek to renew itself. In this perspective, the transformation of territory into landscape, and artwork into the art of gardens, can be related to the intention of establishing systems of places, and making them available to the individual and collective memory.[32]

The Ariadne in the Gardens of Bomarzo is the image of the dream. The world of dreams is that of all dangers. Its entrance is defended by Cerberus, the Whale, and the Dragon. These three guardians prevent the visitor from venturing there recklessly. The labyrinth leads to the union of the three worlds, and to the sources of the evocation of a unitary world. A *mise-en-abyme* of the *Dream of Poliphilus*, the Bomarzo labyrinth may henceforth initiate the walker to the mystery of knowledge and life. An immense mouth opens up, it is the entrance to the underground world. "All thought flies away" says the mouth of shadow, reminiscent of Plato's cave: the knowledge that depends only on sensations resembles that which a prisoner can have, chained in the back of a cave, with his back to the light. He can only know the shadows of objects, projected from the outside on the cave walls. The true aspect of these objects, as they appear in the full light of the sun, escapes the prisoner cut off from the senses. In order to perceive the world, we must construct representations of it, memory palaces. Passing through the grotto offers the possibility of being reborn. Leaving the grotto is accompanied by a sort of bedazzlement by the sun. The

[32] Sébastien Marot, *L'art de la mémoire, le territoire et l'architecture*, (Paris: Editions de la Villette, 2010).

metamorphosis is accomplished. The mouth at Bomarzo is a *camera obscura* that is not limited to the technical assistance it can provide to art. The walker can at last enter the cave of myth, and admire the prodigy that it engendered, the reflection of a world whose reproduction enabled access to forgotten knowledge.

### *Idleness, Arcades, and Poetic Deviations*

In the nineteenth century, it was the city that became the world stage. Henceforward, the street captured every gaze. The *flâneur* wandered through Parisian arcades, went to exhibitions, and discovered panoramas and museums. Nineteenth century humans were inscribed in the urban landscape at the same time as it was inscribed in them. The urban landscape modified walkers, and their behavior and gait. A century later, Walter Benjamin would set himself an incommensurable task: to draw up a heterogeneous inventory of this nineteenth century passion for nonchalant observation. In his book *The Arcade Project*, he transformed the covered passages of Paris, in particular the Passage des Panoramas where Daguerre had his studio, into a sort of collective camera obscura, in which each person is in turn observer and observed, at the center of a casual stage design appropriate for creating associations and ideas. The covered passage was no longer entirely the private internal space, but neither was it the unlimited external space of an invented landscape. This in-between generated an anonymous closeness, a moving theater of operations where situations could take shape. Liandrat-Guigues comments that Baudelaire's *Parisian Scenes* are not realistic:

> they compose a phantasmagoria of brief observations, revealing the invisible when they anatomize the street, tear the

> veil from the crowd and exhibit the hidden image of it. Light and decomposition of movement, uneven flickering of the visible world, support this crisis of representation in the poet, who by way of chronophotography strives to enable the coming of the cinematographic view.[33]

A new way of living together emerged during the nineteenth century. New possibilities for inhabiting, strolling, and meeting people were born out of the construction of artificial atmospheres. Strolling led to specific urban developments: boulevards, covered passages, and gardens (for example the Parc des Buttes Chaumont in Paris). Wandering was promoted to the rank of an artistic approach, broadening the walker's perception far beyond the simple enjoyment of perspectives. The random, letting down one's guard, and the attraction for poetic deviation, were incarnated in idleness and strolling. Baudelaire's *flâneur* meanders, wide-awake, through a city, and revives the functions of the ancient memory palaces: the highly emotional interconnection of places, thoughts, and images. The aim of wandering was no longer to place precise thoughts and images in particular places. The stroll was no longer the journey of a singular individual who could be represented by the mnemonist, the traveler, the peddler, or the pilgrim. The *flâneur* had nothing to hide, and had neither aim nor function. Wandering was a justification in itself, and found its own objective in itself, thus opening up all the links to all the other purely speculative activities of the nineteenth century: photography, the scientific process, and the methodological study of movement that would lead to chronophotography, and then quickly to cinema. Film physically introduced movement into the image right at the time when the idea of movement appeared in the conceptual field, as Benjamin suggested:

[33] Suzanne Liandrat-Guigues, *Esthétique du mouvement cinématographique,* (Paris: Klincksieck, 2005).

> By close-ups of the things around us, by focusing on hidden details of familiar objects, by exploring common place milieus under the ingenious guidance of the camera, the film, on the one hand, extends our comprehension of the necessities which rule our lives; on the other hand, it manages to assure us of an immense and unexpected field of action. Our taverns and our metropolitan streets, our offices and furnished rooms, our railroad stations and our factories appeared to have us locked up hopelessly. Then came the film and burst this prison-world asunder by the dynamite of the tenth of a second, so that now, in the midst of its far-flung ruins and debris, we calmly and adventurously go traveling.[34]

Wandering created film image by image. While wandering appears as one of the essential processes that anticipated and continued the invention of cinema, it was also because, during the nineteenth century, the city became the favorite place to wander. We can imagine the rustic beginnings of music and painting, and indeed that is how they were seen in mythology: for the former, a shepherd playing a reed pipe, and for the latter, a young woman in-love tracing the profile of her lover by the light of a candle. But, as Dominique Noguez remarks, "the beginnings of cinema cannot be conceived outside or without the city." It was the city, and the wanderings it gave rise to, which would create the first tracking shots and its first natural setting. Dziga Vertov showed us that the new memory palaces were no longer isolated, private buildings, but the cities themselves. During the course of the nineteenth and then the twentieth century, new concepts accompanied the genesis of moving images, including the notions of *flânerie* (Benjamin) and

[34] Walter Benjamin, *The Work of Art in the Age of Mechanical Reproduction*, trans. Harry Zohn, (Paris, New York: Schocken/Random House, 1969).

*forme-bal(l)ade*[35] (Deleuze), the idea of the *morality of the tracking shot* (Godard) or the *montage of attractions* (Eisenstein), the distinction between *depth of field* (Bazin) and *perspective* in the history of art, the thinking of *rhizomatic growth* (Guattari and Deleuze), the concept of *flow* (Serres), and *movement of the world* (Schefer).

[35] Deleuze combined the French words forme (form), balade (walk, ride, drive trip, outing ...), and ballade (ballad) to convey the double effect of the tracking shot, both journey and narrative. In English, one might say the walk-ballad form.

Planisphere According to Ptolemy, *Harmonia Macrocosmica,* Andreas Cellarius, 1660.

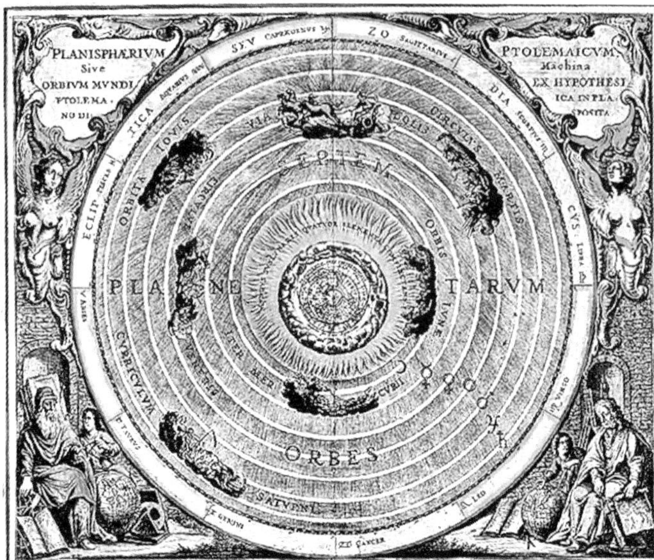


*Cartography of a Geocentric and then Heliocentric World*

The Ptolemaic system reigned supreme in Western thinking for fourteen centuries. During the Renaissance, a handful of men set astronomy on a new path. In 1543, with *De Revolutionibus Orbium Coelestium*, Copernicus sounded the end of egocentrism. Henceforward, it would be the Sun at the center of the system, the Earth being ranked as a planet, turning on its own axis in twenty-four hours, and taking a year to travel its orbit around the Sun. Shortly afterwards, Newton would establish that the forces of attraction that govern the movements of the planets were one and the same as the gravity that governs the falling of terrestrial bodies.

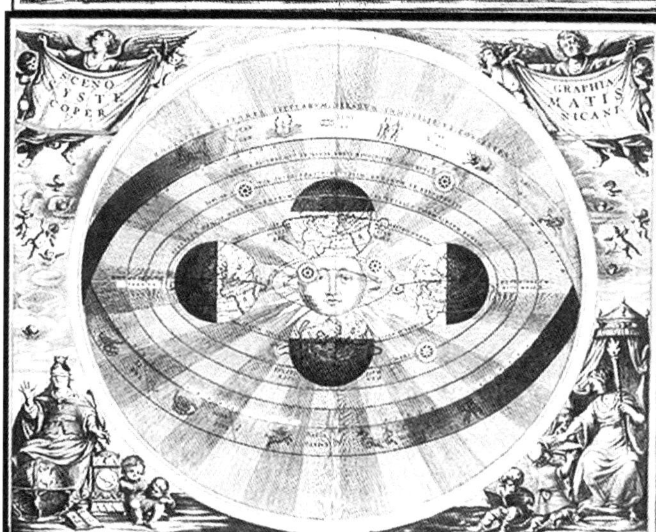

Copernicus's Heliocentric System, *Harmonia Macrocosmica,* Andreas Cellarius, 1660.

# SETTING IMAGES IN MOTION

> **O**n the ceiling of Altamira, in the rooms of Lascaux and Niaux, and in the Val Camonica are carved the incredible beginnings of Art and representation, the results of laborious daydreaming so fertile in images, and the roots of which are so profound that André Breton remarked "*you cannot believe your eyes*."[36]

The question of representation often intersects with the issues touched upon in each epoch by the arts of memory. In the ninth century, Christ was not an image but an incarnation, a representation, and the image of Christ was thus the representation of a representation. In the sixteenth century, in the Garden of Bomarzo, the giant figure is neither an image nor an imitation, but a double. In the ancient *xenia*, the Greek concept of hospitality, which designates, by extension, the gifts given to those to whom we offer hospitality, artifice joins with nature, which it supplants or replaces. In the digital arts of the twenty-first century, we find a similar consideration of space as the product of mental activity, a place of virtual possibilities in terms of movement. Moreover, the same is true in medieval scenography, in which the symbolic quality of the objects represented, determines the situation, the grandeur, and the

[36] Guy Chapouillie, "L'autre séparation," *Entrelacs 5* (Nov. 2005).

relations between them. All of these processes are closer to computer-generated images than to those of the Renaissance based on perspective.

> Between the appearance of a printed culture during the Renaissance and the emergence of the new interactive media at the end of the twentieth century, a cultural parenthesis had become progressively established, in which the intellectual elites had come to consider that writing (especially in its printed form) was the *media princeps* of access to knowledge, and even more so almost the only tool of logical reasoning.[37]

In the cognitive labyrinth between the *xenia* and the digital age, we must perhaps consider Renaissance perspective as a kind of temporary junction, and go back to the paths traced in Byzantium, and during the Middle Ages and the Baroque.

Indeed, toward the end of the sixteenth century, at the dawn of the Baroque period, various experiments with dynamic processes in painting would quickly develop just as the universe was being set into motion. Our view of the universe was being completely modified, which would durably modify questions relating to representation. In spite of the torture of Giordano Bruno and the abjuration of Galileo, Copernicus precipitated the end of geocentrism, and Newton established the identity between the forces of attraction that govern the movements of the planets and the gravity that governs the fall of terrestrial bodies. The distinction between the terrestrial world and the rest of the universe collapsed. In 150 years, between 1543 and 1687, everything changed; the immobile universe was set in motion like a merry-go-round. The emerging centrifugal forces did not only move matter. The images

[37] Henri Hudrisier, "Cicéron aurait-il préconisé le cédérom dans *De oratore?*" *Nouvelles technologies et arts de la mémoire*, (Paris: éditions 00h00, 2002).

born when the world had been immobile, fell off the earth-vehicle as soon as it was set into motion. Schefer writes that "it will have been necessary for the earth to start turning,"[38] for images to do as much.

### *Xenia and Emancipation from the Real*

Representation is specific to humanity. A system of representation consists in gazing *at*, but is also *a moment of* the reality that produces it. If we withdraw from reality the representations that we have of it, where will the rest be, the remainder that reality would be? The link created between the real and its image, is a living, moving, physical link, which creates the real while emancipating itself from it. To describe this phenomenon, the Greeks invented the term *ekphrasis* (from *phrazô*, enable understanding, and *ek*, until the end), the art of the painstaking description of a work of art, a description that should be continued until the subject has been completely and definitively expressed. "It is no longer in ekphrasis a matter of imitating painting, insofar as it seeks to place the object in front of our eyes - painting the object as in a tableau - but of imitating painting as a mimetic art: to paint painting."[39] Diderot would renew with this tradition in the eighteenth century in his *Salon* reviews. His reviews were written for a journal copied by hand, the *Literary Correspondence*, which as it was not printed, was able to avoid censorship, and could dare to adopt a tone, a style, and express ideas very freely, renewing in particular with the Platonic idea according to which painting is a *representation of representation*.

This kind of experience went even further with the *xenia*, these gifts, delicacies, or fruit baskets, sent as presents by hosts to their

[38] Jean-Louis Schefer, *Du monde et du mouvement des images*, (Paris: Cahiers du Cinéma), 1997.
[39] Barbara Cassin, *L'effet sophistique,* (Paris: Gallimard, 1995).

guests, the day after a dinner party. These delicacies were often the same as those served at the dinner party the previous evening. The host often added a painting that represents the sending of these fine foods. The guests of the previous evening could thus taste again some of the meal items and also keep a pictorial trace of it. This image of this twofold moment hovers between the time of yesterday's meal, the partial repetition of it, and the memory of these two moments. This image is already no longer a simple figuration of the real; by giving meaning to the passing of time, it moves toward a form of symbolization. In addition to this doubling by an image, sometimes came the doubling by a text, when the host took on a role as a writer and joined a written description of the painting offered. A strange modernity characterizes the *xenia*, due to their degree of emancipation from the real. The representation in the text or image is not meant to imitate the real, but rather to partake of the real, or play with it. The same is true in medieval scenography, in which the symbolic quality of the objects represented, determines the situation, grandeur of, and relations between them. This process was more of a precursor of computer-generated images than Renaissance perspective. Indeed, in the digital arts, one finds the same considerations of space as the product of mental activity and a place of the virtual possibilities of motion.

The ambiguity of representation is central to the divergence in the status of the image that separates Eastern and Western traditions. For pagan philosophers in late Antiquity, the body is no more than an external envelope. Its representation is therefore only the appearance of an appearance—the dead image of an ephemeral body. For Christians, the image is not only a medium that is too material to adequately express the Divine, it is similar to an idol and is thus in contradiction with a major taboo in the Old Testament.

Toward the fifth century, two roads diverged. In the West, Saint Augustine explained that one can love without imagining, and that, in the absence of evidence, we can imagine Christ with the traits suggested by our own psychology, or our own memory work. In the East, theology placed the painted images of religious scenes at the lowest level in the hierarchy of resemblances, much lower than writing, which has the advantage of being immaterial. Images were considered to be the book of the illiterate, tolerable but not recommendable. A slow process of maturation of over a century would be necessary, in what would be called the iconoclastic crisis, for these images, which were rather scorned, to be placed at the highest level in this hierarchy, and called the Son in the image of the Father, and man in the image of God.

Byzantine Iconoclasm caused bloodshed in Byzantium in the eighth and ninth centuries (730–843), officially ending in 843 when icon-veneration was re-established. This was a peculiar time during which the status of the image became a question of life or death, exile, and destruction. Can the divine principle be represented in a visible form? The *iconoclasts* argued no, because a material form betrays the essence of the divinity, and by proposing the illusion of a resemblance, makes people take the sign for the thing, which leads to idolatry. The *iconodules* argued yes, because when God was incarnated as Jesus Christ he became visible, and he can thus be represented. For the iconoclasts, it is an image *in the likeness of*, and for the iconodules an image *produced for*. The iconoclasts believed that any image is the expression of a fallacious substitution. On the contrary, the iconodules argue that Christ, the image of the Father, is identical to him in essence, and yet he is the incarnation of Him, the image in flesh. In other words, the icon has a model, which is already an image, an invisible likeness. This speculative basis theoretically prevents icons from being mixed up with idols. The iconodules introduced another way of analyzing the status of images, which constitutes the "genesis of a way of thinking about images we inherited."[40]

### *Phantasms, Paintings that Speak, and Theaters of Memory*

The Romans conflated the dead with the image. The corpse is what has the same figure. The dead are the quintessential *imago*, while the *imago* was above all the image of the dead. The *imagines* were wax masks of the ancestors that noble Romans displayed in the atriums of their homes. In the funerary rituals of many peoples, the first effect of death is to transform the dead into *phantasms*, or what the Greeks called *eidolon*; that is, a vague and threatening being that remains in the world of the living and returns to the places formerly used by the deceased. The aim of these funerary rituals is indeed to transform this cumbersome being into an ancestor; in other words, into an image, but one that is beneficial and separated from the world of the living.

> Things get clearer as soon as the image is qualified in its relation with the subject, at the crossroads of gazing and exchanging, and with the circulation of signs (distinct from the commerce of things), with what I call the commerce of gazes. It is the gaze of the subject that gives the image its status as *eikon* or *eidolon*, *fantasmata, fantasma.* It is how the gaze is constructed that reifies or does not reify the object.[41]

The doctrine on the relationship between the visible and the invisible is an unprecedented opening for meditations on vision and the gaze. It is an exceptional speculative system vis-à-vis the

[40] Marie-José Mondzain, *Image, icône, économie : Les sources byzantines de l'imaginaire contemporain*, (Paris: Seuil, 1996).
[41] Marie-José Mondzain, interview with Michaela Fiserova, *Sens Public*, (2007).

question of contemplation, and the relations between knowledge and belief. In this quest related to visibilities and creation, language and image take initiatives successively. In the first memory palaces, images became preferably *active beings* (*imagines agentes*); that is, they struck the imagination. In the Byzantium of the eighth and ninth centuries, the image became an *icon*, by being produced as an artificial image. By renewing the status of the image, Byzantium made possible for the first time ever the operation of artificial substitution based on what Bruno would develop as the notion of *phantasm*. Indeed, he did not employ the arts of memory only as a mnemotechnical device, but also as a veritable machine for *manipulating* — in the proper sense of *putting one's hand on* — *phantasms* and *images*. For Bruno, if humans should be placed at the center of a cosmogony, it is not because of their intellectual superiority, but because of their aptitude for *manual* activity. Magical operations reveal the secret nature of the real, if we can only explain how they function. According to Bruno, the magical art is the art of acting upon human imagination. Through "bonds", it links the techniques for creating, manipulating, and communicating about imaginary universes and personal mythologies. Several mechanisms enable these links to be established, through words and songs, incantations, as well as the images and signs imprinted in human memory. In Bruno's system, imagination, and more precisely animated imagination, is the source of psychic energy. Compared to the ancient memory palaces, the status and the name of the images have changed; they are no longer *imagines*, but *phantasmata* (from *phantasms)*. The real nourishes the human imagination through phantasms, and in turn the imagination gives form to the real. The imagination functions as a kind of guidance system for the real, continually providing the mind with a vision of the world. Language only enables us to describe the finite elements of the world, but not the world in its overall form. To arrive at this second level of comprehension, Bruno tried to create a meta-language for manipulating phantasms, which would open the way to manipulating the real itself. This movement, which navigates between the image and the phantasm, is more of an art than a science, and this art would dominate all the fantastic undertakings from the Middle Ages to the Renaissance, including the arts of memory, magic, alchemy, the *Cabala*, and the art of gardens.

The principles of linear perspective theorized in Leon Battista Alberti's treatise, *De Pictura* (1435), represent a decisive development in the history of the status of the image. For the first time ever, the painted image is envisaged within a comprehensive system, analogous to that of the written language, with its own grammar, alphabet, syntax, and semantics. It could be analyzed and defined in terms of basic notions and rules. Therefore, it is no longer a matter of speculation, chance, or fantasy, but rather of rational knowledge. The goal was to define the parameters of the variations in the characteristics of the geometrical plane or perspectival cone to create an art of illusion. Until the fourteenth century, sacred paintings were brimming with coded notations that were not accessible to everyone. The function of these codes is related to the arts of memory. To read these signs, it was first necessary to know them. The Renaissance is marked by a change with respect to the simple reading of these signs. The image must not only be a memory aid for a religious doctrine, displaying a collection of signs and recalling the twists and turns of a scenario, it must also convince and move people. The image must deliver a message. Paintings start to speak.

The work of Pieter Aertsen, and later of Velázquez, mark a phase of extreme meta-pictorial tension. The paintings of Pieter

Aertsen were completed before the explosion of the iconoclastic crisis in the Netherlands in 1566; however, they were ahead of their time in addressing the controversial issues concerning images. The new status of the image inaugurated by the Reformation would result in an extremely polarized situation. The walls in the Netherlands and northern Europe were becoming blank, while in Italy, Spain, and central Europe, they were being covered with trompe-l'œil paintings. It is no coincidence that in parallel to the emergence in Flanders of the pictorial genre of painted galleries, the genre of church interiors, in which immaculate white is the dominant theme of the image, became crystallized in Calvinist Holland. Yet among the Reformers, there was no theory of art, only a theory of the image and of the sign. Art theory was the prerogative of the South. This nascent theory does not focus on the purpose of the image, but on the ultimate goal of art, on the creation of the great mnemotechnical systems of artistic knowledge. The appearance of *art history* is undoubtedly its most important invention.

Art history was veritably born in 1550 with the first edition of Vasari's *Lives of the Most Excellent Painters, Sculptors, and Architects, from Cimabue to Our Times*. Some thirty years later, this historical approach would be succeeded by the theoretical work of Gian Paolo Lomazzo from Milan, who recomposed the artistic theory of the arts of memory. Lomazzo invented an imaginative system, which enables the most valid artistic solutions to be combined in the creation of the perfect work of art. This grand machine is called the *temple of painting*, an imaginary construction based on the model of Giulio Camillo's *Theater of Memory*. For Camillo and Lomazzo, no individual can approach perfection, only a combinatory art can come close. By selecting and combining the talents of different artists, one may achieve the perfect work.

*Selectio* and *combinatio* are not attitudes of the artist facing the real, but facing art. In fact, all of the inventions potentially present in the temple of painting are all the possible combinations of pictorial language. The temple is a grand edifice for memory, and at the same time a grand machine for the imagination.

Lomazzo's mnemotechnical temple would be embodied, as of the early Baroque, in the architectural practice of the *studiolo*, which was the prince's private study. It was a closed room with no windows, and on its walls there were paintings that traced the history and knowledge of the world. It was a space isolated from the real world, but open to the abstract space of memory. The *studiolo* contained the entire world painted on its walls. The one of Francesco I de' Medici in the Palazzo Vecchio of Florence (1570-73) was designed as a coherent system of places (its cabinets) and images (the paintings adorning their doors). It was in the shape of a jewelry box, and contained the rarest and most precious pieces in his collection. The paintings themselves represented a sort of inventory of the things kept behind them. During the second half of the fourteenth century, the *studiolo*, curiosity cabinets, painting-encrusted walls, and *cabinets d'amateur* were created based on the combinatory criteria of the *ars inveniendi* and *combinandi* of Camillo, which are criteria directly inherited from the arts of memory. This conception of art constitutes the final rampart against the obliteration of images that would take place as of the Reformation.

The Renaissance was the very moment in which language supplanted the image. This autonomization of language is astutely described by Foucault in *The Order of Things*. The place-image relations in the ancient arts of memory were profoundly transformed by this process, as the setting in motion of images corresponded to a questioning of places. In the sixteenth century, the genre of the tableau started to make the painting its own subject. The frame shows that things are being shown, without absorption or immersion. The theatrical space underwent the same developments as the pictorial frame. What is suggested is a certain convergence of the history of painting and the history of theater, towards the notion of the scene, as both scene and stage. The scenic conception of theatrical space is derived from the perspectival organization of space, but also from the scenarios inherent in the arts of memory. The search for particular correspondences between places and images opened up the way to a differential semantization of places according to the scenes depicted, and reciprocally a cross-contamination of the scenes by their frames. In this hypothetical development, the arts of memory will have played a role in the growing distinction between scenes (tragic, satirical, and comic), and genre (pictorial, literary…), resulting in a kind of insertion of images in places. The stage in theater and the frame in painting materialize the very figure of the representation of space, with the establishment of the notions of *outside the frame* in painting and the *backstage* in theater.

In the early sixteenth century, the court masque started to lose its ephemeral character. It would take place inside the palace, in a permanent theater designed for that purpose. About 1589, the engineer Bernado Buontalenti was commissioned by the Medicis in Florence to artificially revive the mythical universe of Antiquity. He refurbished the former Uffizi Theater, in which he installed machines, adapted the infrastructure to producing hitherto unseen special effects, and above all added a framed proscenium to the original stage design. This separation between the stage and the audience marked a new phase in the history of theater design: using the imaginary surface suggested by the arch, it enabled an illusionary space to be constructed by playing on the effects of perspective. In 1947, in an article about three dimensions in film, Sergei Eisenstein saw the invention of the *proscenium* as one of the first manifestations of cinematographic space, while Aby Warburg recognized in the nature of Renaissance feasts and masques a form of transition between the real and representation.

### *Intertextual Images and Dynamic Narration*

Between theater and what would become cinema, lies the whole history of space in painting to be read: its decentering, illimitation, and explosion. In *L'instauration du tableau*, Victor Stoïchita describes how, between 1522 and 1675 in Europe, the tableau vivant made the image appear as an image, in other words as meaningful:

> by contrast with former images, linked to a precise religious function and a particular place, the tableau is an object that is defined neither by its liturgical function nor by being exhibited in a fixed place. Its appearance in the late Renaissance coincides with the awareness of painting as such, with the birth of the modern conception of the artist.[42]

Opposed in particular to the mystical function of the icon, the tableau led to a major change in visual expression and the theories of representation.

By comparison with painting, which until then had been essentially religious, the tableau introduced a new form of narrative, leading in turn to a new way of looking.

The innovation is to present an *intertextual* image, in other words an image endowed with its own autonomy, offering a

[42] Victor I Stoïchita, *L'instauration du tableau*, diss. Sorbonne, 1989 (Geneva: Droz, 2003).

> combinatorial interlocution to the *viewer* through multiple layers of meaning. What Stoichita calls the intertextual relationship is the appeal to the viewer to proceed independently, with no preexisting syntax, to combine the significations embedded in the image.[43]

If, in the canvas, the sequence of views makes up the text, this effect would be continued in the contemporary form of the image, the moving image.

The frescos painted around 1425 by Masaccio, Masolino, and Philippino Lippi in the Brancacci Chapel of the Santa Maria del Carmine Church in Florence introduced dynamic narration into painting. In *Expulsion from the Garden of Eden*, Masaccio represented the characters walking, with their feet solidly planted on the ground and all the weight of humanity on their backs. They are no longer stiff and floating as in the Byzantine pictorial tradition. In *The Tribute Money*, the subject is represented as an indeterminate immeasurable space. Masaccio painted using the same technique as Poussin, Monet, and Cézanne: he used color to construct shape. Through Masaccio, in the early Quattrocento, art was renewed by substituting truly pictorial values for the dominant values of volume.

When Paolo Uccello completed *The Battle of San Romano*, around 1450, he too was seeking a certain dynamic in painting, organizing the progression of movement by scanning from one side to the other. From right to left, the knights's lances are progressively lowered from vertical to horizontal. Horses, weapons, and knights are superimposed in the various phases of the attack, with their entanglement creating a blurred effect that is very close to how rapid movement is captured in a photograph taken at a slow shutter

[43] Olivier Bomsel and Jean-Charles Blais, "L'apparition du DVD," History and Economy of Digitization Seminar, Cerna Ecole des Mines, EHESS, 2004.

speed. This attempt to represent movement, and therefore time, in the two-dimensional universe of painting was an exceptional approach at that time, when the main preoccupation was the representation of space through perspective. *The Battle of San Romano* anticipated by four centuries the deconstruction of movement in the photographs of Etienne-Jules Marey, and later in the paintings of Marcel Duchamp.

Ghirlandaio's frescos in the Sassetti Chapel of the Santa Trinita Church in Florence (1485) are among the first scenographic documents in Italian painting, aimed at speculation and self-contemplation. The space depicted opens on the surroundings of the church so that the space of the Sassetti Chapel seems to turn inside out like a glove. The surface of the frescos works like a reverse window that opens not on an imaginary or distant land, but on the real exterior of the Santa Trinita Church, in a process strangely similar to the camera obscura. Entering the church and walking toward Ghirlandaio's frescos, the spectator goes seamlessly from the view of the real town to that of its representation, returning to the world by way of images.

But it was in Antwerp, around 1550, that a new way of conceptualizing the pictorial image appeared: the inverted still life. Its initiator was Pieter Aertsen, who had been deeply shaken by the destruction of his paintings by iconoclastic Protestants. These works are images that have the image as their theme. The painting *Christ in the House of Martha and Mary* is a still life in which the artist has inserted a tableau vivant. Three of the objects in the still life in the foreground spill over into the doorway in the middle ground. In the background, on the third flagstone in the far left of the picture, there is an inscription: *Luke 10*. The background is an allegorical representation of a text from the Gospel. The painting is to be read, starting from the floor of the narrow corridor situated where all reading begins—on the left. The gaze is invited to shift progressively from left to right in a horizontal *pan shot*. Yet Aertsen clearly indicates that the reading should be continued in the background: By having the leg of lamb encroach upon the doorway, he shows that at the point at which the biblical text ends another text begins, this time not made up of letters and words, but objects. In comparison with the background image, it is the foreground that is like an inset illustration, an effect accentuated by its irreligious character. The background is a text translated into an image; it is sacred in character and makes use of the traditional features of painting. Meanwhile, the foreground is an anti-image; using the methods of a different art, it shows an illustration that is irreligious in character. This process could be called a backward *tracking shot*, including in the visual field things that are usually outside the frame, a part of the viewer's space, in other words far removed from the image.

*The Mnemosyne Project,* Aby Warburg 1926.

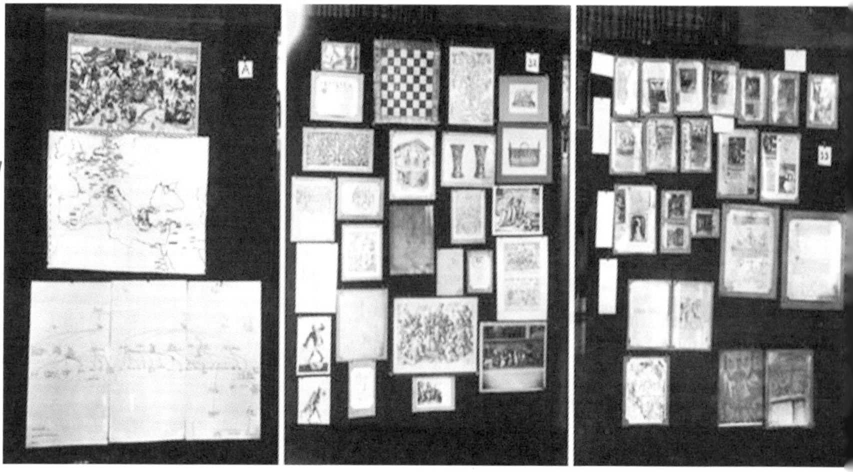

*Map of an anthropocentered artistic creation*

During the first century of the Baroque period, between the end of the sixteenth and the beginning of the seventeenth century, an increasing number of experiments with dynamic processes in painting (dynamic narration, appeal for a mobile gaze, ...) would occur in response to the universe being set in motion. Our reading of the universe was being completely transformed, which would result in long-term changes to issues of representation. Images take life in the studiolo of Renaissance Florence, as in the twentieth century in Aby Warburg's Mnemosyne project, which was supposed to be a gigantic condenser of all of the currents of energy in Europe.
Studiolo of Francesco I – Palazzo Vecchio, Florence, 1572.

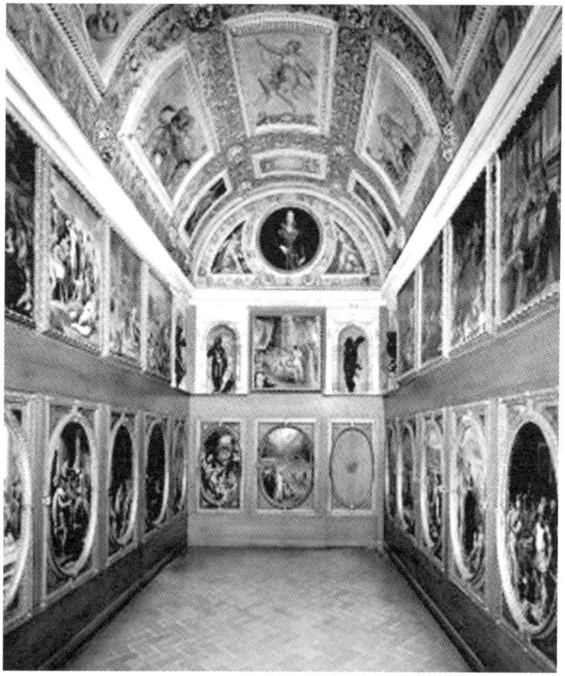

*Studiolo of Francesco I* – Palazzo Vecchio – Florence 1572

**B**y incessantly linking and unlinking their forces in human inventions, language and the image have marked their territories in every era. Places maintain traces of these ongoing transformations, and have evolved from the most strictly personal to the most collective. In every period, place-thought-image links have deeply transformed the status of places and images. The seventeenth century of Giordano Bruno definitely represents a sort of climax in these interactions, before the late Reformation and the rise of the printing press opened a long period of obscurity for the arts of memory.

It is, however, in seeking new ways to link images and language that the inner fire of the arts of memory could remain smoldering, and flare up again at the end of the nineteenth century. For, in order to develop successfully, the arts of memory have always given priority to the language-image relation, going as far as actually fusing them: imagining spaces, and then walking in and attaching mental images to them. It is not a static arrangement, but an interconnection, a journey of the mind among images; and we know today that memory is not a deposit, but rather a network of connections. Already, in ancient Greece, people memorized music by linking musical phrases to the corporeal movements of dance.

This combination of dance and music was called *mousikê*. To these links, the arts of memory added the importance of the *interactions* between the audio and the visual, the eye that listens, and the ear that sees—a sophisticated alchemy that would directly inspire Dziga Vertov, and which is central to contemporary multimedia creation.

It is through these interactions that the arts of memory succeeded so well in *putting the world into people's heads*, by opening and developing two inseparable orientations that nourish the contemporary arts today. The first gives priority to the combination and arrangement of non-representative signs, letters or figures, the other to images as if they were the best mnemonic helpers. On the one hand, the *matrix* (tables of correlations, hierarchies, and the organized arrangement of data); on the other, *theater* (places inhabited by images and thoughts, scenarios, and interactivity). A *combinatory art* and a *figurative art*. These two occurrences of thought and representation emerged in the Middle Ages and during the Renaissance. They first crossed paths with each other during the Baroque period, before prefiguring the arrival of images in motion and the emergence of the digital arts.

### *Animated Figures, Monads, and the Camera Obscura*

Having reached a high point with the scholastic philosophers of the thirteenth century, the arts of memory stopped developing or grew strange new limbs. In the sixteenth century, illustrious intellectuals, from Erasmus to Melanchton, and Agrippa to Rabelais, critiqued and satirized of them. Little by little, memory images degenerated into pious images. The development of the arts of memory was suddenly arrested in the seventeenth century, when Bruno was burned at the stake in Campo dei Fiori. Campanella himself barely escaped from such a fate, and the Jesuit priest Matteo Ricci would not return from China. The witch hunt in Europe was in full swing, "the theater of the world was breaking up to form various scenes, and the theater of memory was no longer able to reunite and represent it."[44] With the invention of the printing press, the sophisticated mnemonic devices started losing their importance. As a result of these major changes, images would become the official domain of the field of art while the book would become the depository of knowledge. Image and language were no longer bound to memory, and thereafter followed separate paths.

In response to the art of memory based on places and images, the Protestant culture of the Renaissance attempted to impose a mnemotechnical system without icons. The codification of perspective and the invention of printing contributed to the dissolution of the mental representations that link places, images, and thoughts. The analogical correspondence between gothic architecture and scholastic thought was compromised, and the arts of memory were equated with the Middle Ages. During the Renaissance, logical analysis, the order of texts, and summaries typographically organized on the page, were the only tools used for memorization. The birth of the printing press laid the foundations of a world in which memory was going to progressively lose its importance, until it would become practically useless. While historians argue that the Reformation was partly due to the invention of printing, they rarely highlight the importance of the Reformation in the development of iconoclasm in the eighteenth century. Because of the Reformation's battle against the cult of idols, iconic

[44] Lina Bolzoni, "The Play of Images: the Art of Memory from Its Origins to the Seicento," *The Enchanted Loom: Chapters in the History of Neuroscience,* (Oxford: Oxford UP, 1991) (our trans. from the French).

representations were removed from places of worship, and the imagination was long censored. Phantasms, as defined by Bruno, were rejected as if they were productions of personal idols. Thereafter, the very foundations of the arts of memory became marginalized.

It was, however, during the Baroque period, between the end of the sixteenth and the beginning of the seventeenth century, that the arts of memory and private collecting, visible in the *studiolo* then in *cabinets of curiosities,* interacted and exchanged models and techniques, which superimposed mental and physical places, and made the map of the mind correspond with the map of things. In *The Gallery of Memory*, Lina Bolzoni insists on the paradox of this era: whereas the arts of memory emerged in an oral society, it is in the age of the printing press that they burned brightly once again. Losing their initial utility, they gained in rhetorical utility. Printing removed words from the temporal and ephemeral realm of oral communication, and placed them on the space of the page. Written words then became objects, artificial products that last through time, and which could be dissected and analyzed. Thought became matter and could henceforth be located in space, and processes linked to the senses were perceived in terms of movement. Memory was no longer a closed and finite space, but infinitely open. Images enjoyed a new and extraordinary vitality. Language and image tended to be superimposed upon and correspond with each other. The result was the dream of a universal theater, a universal language capable of communicating by means of images, and which would still be valid in the Encyclopedia of Enlightenment philosophers. Two particular figures would mark their era by the extent and diversity of their explorations, Giambattista Vico and Leibniz, who would introduce the arts of memory into modernity.

From his chair as professor of rhetoric, Vico, a Neapolitan philosopher well-versed in the arts of memory, engaged in battle during the early eighteenth century against the spread of the principles of the Cartesian method throughout European thinking. When Descartes tried to describe how universal reason must be deployed, he established a model for a language that operates by means of denotation with respect to the real; that is, in the literal expression of the real. He completely ignored the other facet of language, which enables a thought to be enriched through metaphoric connotations, and individual works to be created through the opening of each word onto various mental images. Contrary to the simple designation of the real advocated by Descartes, Vico believed that humanity grasps the world through a global, immediate, and poetic form of perception, from which we can draw a universal interpretation. Vico calls this work that combines language and imagination *ingegno* in his main book *The New Science*. *Ingegno* enables separate things to be linked rapidly and appropriately. Vico reutilizes the basic ideas in Giulio Camillo's *Theater of Memory* to put into motion the figures, universals, and poetic characters of human society. But far from being a static representation, Vico gave life to these animated figures, which are the story, speak, and are the interpretation of allegories. The things various mythologies had attributed to the gods, Vico tried to represent as the invention by men of their own humanity. In his reformulation of the arts of memory, Vico strives tirelessly to understand how the universal places of human thought are formed. In opposition to the dominant Cartesianism of the time, he realized two centuries before the creations of the nineteenth century that the language of words alone cannot suffice, and that words had to be associated with images.

Leibniz would continue the research for a *world in the head*, present in the *studioli*, and created the notion of *monad* that he would develop in *The Monadology, and* which would be revisited by Deleuze in the twentieth century in *The Fold*. The monad is a minimal conscious entity that has "no windows, through which anything could come in or go out."[45] From the arts of memory to the monad, the processes elaborated are ones based on projection.

> For ages there have been places where what is to be seen is inside: a cell, sacristy, crypt, church, theater, study, or print room. The Baroque explored all of these places to draw power and glory from them. First, the camera obscura has only one small aperture high up through which passes light, then through the relay of two mirrors it projects on a sheet the objects to be drawn that cannot be seen, the second mirror being tilted according to the position of the sheet. Then transformational scenes, painted skies, all kinds of trompe l'œil that adorn the walls: the monad only has trompe l'œil furniture and objects.[46]

Seventeenth century Leibnizians no longer believed in the possibility of representing reality. The Baroque preferred the simulacrum to the imitation of reality. The thread of the labyrinth replaced the chain of knowledge and penetrated the domain of dreams. A dream of cinema took shape. "What the gestures that resemble drowning people in the Baroque world evoke is not a modification of the image; it is rather a succession of images; it is not astonishing that this art of gestures and feelings, which is obsessed with theater, ended up in the cinema."[47] One text, more than any other, illustrates Leibniz's encyclopedic frenzy and

[45] Gottfried Wilhem Leibniz, *The Monadology,* http://philosophy.eserver.org/leibniz-monadology.txt
[46] Gilles Deleuze, *The Fold: Leibniz and the Baroque*, trans. Tom Conley, (London; New York: Continuum, 2006 (our adaptation)).
[47] André Malraux, *Esquisse d'une psychologie du cinéma*, (Nouveau Monde Éditions: Paris, 2003).

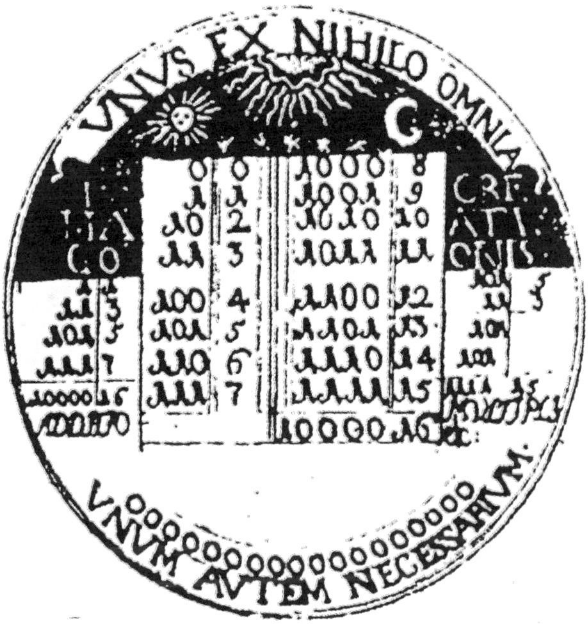


Leibniz's medallion for the Duke of Brunswick (1697).

*Characteristica Universalis*

Among his other creations, Leibniz wrote a text on the arts of memory that was never published. He also invented integral calculus and the binary number system, which is the base of all computing today. It is thus Leibniz who opened the door to computing, which in addition to its computational power and memory, makes it possible to unfold a thought in different ways by means of a file tree for representing reasoning, or a search path.

enthusiasm for inventing new constructions, his *Funny Thought Concerning a New Kind of Representations*:

> One could also attach shadow theatres [...], or a sloping theatre, where at the end of the viewing side there would be a light and small wooden figures, which would be moved so that they cast their shadows on a translucent paper behind which would likewise be a light. In this way, the shadows would appear on the paper in an impressive way in large format. But in order for the shadow figures not all to appear on the same level, the choice of perspective could reduce the size of the shadows. They would wander from the edge to the middle and this would give the impression of coming forwards from the back. They increase in size if they reduce their distance from the light, which is easy and simple to arrange. There would be continuous wonderful metamorphoses, daring leaps and flights. Circe, the sorceress, who transforms emerging hells. All of a sudden everything would be dark: at this point the same wall would be of service again by extinguishing all light apart from that near to the small moving wooden figures. The remaining light with the help of a magic lantern would cast wonderfully beautiful and agile figures against the wall, which would conform to the same law of perspective. All this would be accompanied by a song behind the theatre. The small figures would be operated from below or by their feet, so that whatever serves to move them remains invisible. Song and music would accompany everything.[48]

The Baroque era is thus characterized by an irresistible desire for an art of deception and optical illusions, which is a final resurgence of the first arts of memory, but also an exacerbated form of the magical mechanisms conceived by Bruno.

[48] Gottfried Wilhem Leibniz, *Drôle de pensée touchant une nouvelle sorte de représentation*, English trans. from Helmar Schramm, Ludger Schwarte and Jan Lazardzig eds., Collection, Laboratory, Theater: Scenes of Knowledge in the 17th Century, (Berlin: Walter de Gruyter, 2005), 271.

## *Magic / Image*

The Baroque did not invent cinema, but it did imagine its effects and fundamental issues. The history of the moving image does not begin with cinema, and its issues go well beyond the technological specificities of the medium. Cinema would emerge via a long process, nourished in particular by the arts of memory, which would lead to the convergence of various techniques. Some, like the study of movement, go back to Antiquity and Ptolemy; while others, such as the recording of sound, did not appear until the nineteenth century.

Since Antiquity, humans have continuously sought to encircle the universe and enclose the world in a box. The camera obscura, which has been passed down through the centuries, is certainly one of the most permanent elements in this research that stretches from Plato to Leonardo da Vinci. With his allegory of the cave, Plato did not invent the cinema either, yet the precision of his description of the cinematographic process is quite troubling. The images produced in the camera obscura render movement and extend to everything visible, but remain highly fugitive and irremediably dependent on the presence of their model.

Athanasius Kircher is in the same tradition as thinkers such as Ramon Llull, Giovanni Pico della Mirandola, Marsilio Ficino, and Bruno, within the important Neoplatonic current that combined scientific and philosophical experiments. In 1645, in his book *Ars Magna Lucis et Umbrae*, the Jesuit priest Kircher (1602-1680) lists and describes the optical procedures used from the initial versions of the camera obscura to the first magical lanterns, and he is even considered to be one of the first people to experiment with synesthasia, seeking to link visual sensations and auditive sensations three centuries before the invention du VJing. He revisits Llull's *Ars*

*Combinatoria* in a more complex environment, combining the metaphysics of correspondences and experimentation with sophisticated mechanisms. Kircher also conceived a reconstruction of Noah's ark transformed into a universal system of the art of memory. According to Laurent Mannoni, he is one of the links in the long cinematographic chain, the long series of experimentations on the interconnections linking thoughts and images, a long series of extravagant inventions and increasingly elaborate techniques such as Christian Huygens's *lantern of fright* (1659), Johann Schröpfer's *nebulous lantern* (1774), the phantasmagoria of Étienne-Gaspard Robert (1763-1837), the *fantastic evenings* of Jean Eugène Robert-Houdin (1805-1871), in which a certain Georges Méliès participated, Emile Reynaud's *praxinoscope* (1877), Jules Marey's chronophotographic gun (1882), and Edison's Kinetoscope (1889). From the seventeenth to the nineteenth century, the image became progressively mobile. The same temporal paradox characterizes the animation of memory indexes in Camillo's Theater of Memory, Bruno's magical practices, Vico's allegorical figures, and later the photographic images of Lumière and Méliès:

> the invention of dreaming out loud preceded the invention of the machines that would project these dreams. Here is something that seems to be specific to the nineteenth century: racing over the continents, accompanying the fall of kings, and constituting in the middle of the first industrial steam engines a sort of valve for humanity, dreams suddenly geminate, proliferate, and have a ripple effect, no longer in terms of roles or predictions, but by beginning to show, in the lining of every person, openings to unknown worlds.[49]

[49] Jean-Louis Schefer, *Du monde et du mouvement des images*, (Paris: Cahiers du Cinéma, 1997).

From magic to image, there is always experimentation that feeds imaginary devices and the representations of different universes, which propose as poetic resources the exploration of minute details, durations, modes of sequencing, and different versions of reality.

In 1895, the Lumière brothers continued to build on the achievements of their colleagues and predecessors, such as Marey's sequential images and Edison's perforated film. Their device was reversible and enabled images to be recorded, sorted, and projected. The first private screening was held on March 22, 1895 in Paris for an audience of small business owners. The first public screening took place on December 28, 1895 in the Indian Salon at the Grand Café, Boulevard des Capucines in Paris, with thirty-three ticket buyers for the opening performance, and thousands in the following days.

Yet it is Méliès who most inventively marked this passage from magic to image. A magic enthusiast and magician himself, Méliès was very familiar with the techniques of the magic lantern, which had long been part of shows involving conjuring. Méliès attended this first historical public screening in December 1895. He would revolutionize this emerging art, going from reports to fiction, accentuating the effects of staging, creating the first cinema studio in the world, and inventing special effects. While filming some of his first images at the Place de l'Opéra in Paris with his experimental camera, the film jammed in the reel. He stopped the shooting, reloaded the film, and then resumed the shooting. When he developed the film, on the square occupied by vehicles, he saw a bus transformed into a hearse. Remembering this incident, he would invent the *conjuring away* of one view by another, by means of direct editing while filming. Film a character. Stop filming. Remove the character from the frame. Refilm. On the screen, the character will

Projected images – *Ars Magna Lucis et Umbrae* – Athanasius Kircher (1646)

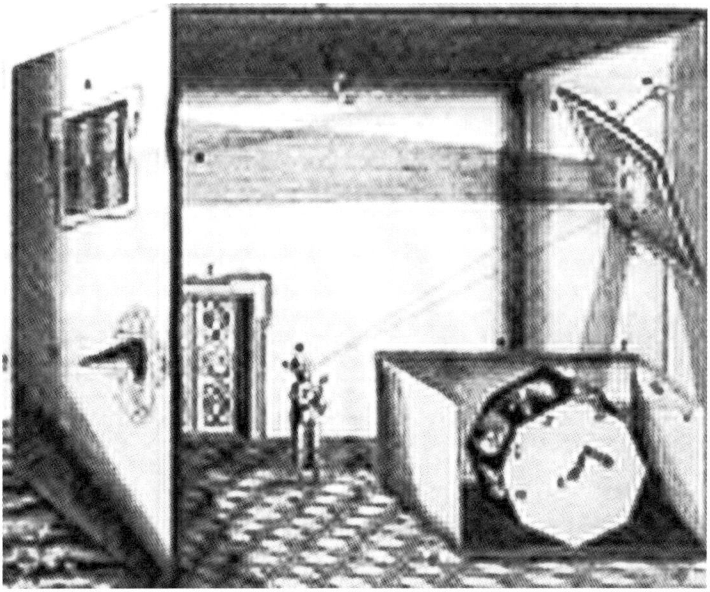

*The Realm of Dreams*
In the tradition of Giordano Bruno, Kircher experimented with the interactions of thought and matter. His optical research would find an unexpected extension in what was called the art of deception, as in Kircher's machinery in which those who look into a mirror see the head of an animal instead of their own, or later in Emile Reynaud's praxinoscope.

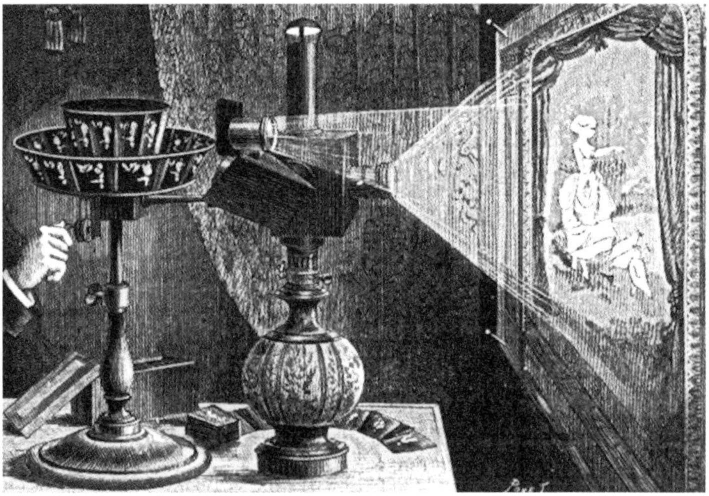

Praxinoscope, Emile Reynaud, Paris (1877).

disappear. The first cinematographic special effects had been invented.

*Illusion, Casting Shadows, and Cinema*

If cinema, according to Bazin, was "always present in the Platonic sky," Jean-Louis Schefer argues that it seems to have emerged in the universe full of atoms of the pre-Socratic philosophers who conceived the first memory palaces. Subjecting the movement of bodies to the general pulverization of the objects of the world, the grain of cinema is all that moves:

> the movement produced by the gazes and the bodies of the spectators scrutinizing a painting, is now in the movie camera, among things. The possibility of advancing one's gaze (*zooming in*), of moving closer or farther (*tracking*), and of turning or raising the head (*panning*) has been passed into the body of the movie camera.[50]

In Méliès's 1895 system, cinema consists in capturing then projecting photographic images set in motion. This combination of different techniques makes it a hybrid invention, which raises the problem of its genealogy. Notably in France, the ontological conception of cinema, derived from the Bazin's arguments, was such that the projection of images was devalued while the photographic reproduction of the real was championed. For example, Deleuze argues that

> When we think about the prehistory of cinema, we sometimes end up confused, because we do not know where its technological tradition begins, or how to define the tradition that characterizes it. We can always refer to shadow puppets,

[50] André Habib, "L'œil détaillé," *Hors-Champ*, (2002).

> or the most ancient projection systems. However, the determining conditions of cinema are the following: not merely the photo, but the snapshot (studio photography belongs to the other tradition); the equidistance of the snapshots; the transfer of this equidistance onto the medium that constitutes the "film" (it was Edison and Dickson who perforated film); a mechanism for advancing images (the Lumière claw)[51]

In other words, for Deleuze the invention of cinema is completely based on the inventions of *photography* (the snapshot) and *setting it into motion* (a device for creating a regular succession of photographs). However, in his conception, a third essential invention of cinema is relegated to the background, which is the *projection* of images (in the *technical* as well as the *oneiric* sense of the term). For in cinema, photograph and projection are inextricable, and indeed this duality is strengthened and galvanized by motion. Insofar as it is photography, cinema conserves a trace of the real, at least of a real that *has undeniably been*, as Roland Barthes would have it. Insofar as it is projection, cinema cuts itself off from the real to present in its place and on a blank surface, shadows of immaterial and phantomatic images. From photography, the cinematographer Lumière was born, with his ambition to establish a double of reality. From projection came the cinematographer Méliès, and his world of appearances and disappearances. Together, these two matrixes shaped the codes of the cinema of fiction, establishing the bases of the cinematograhic image therein as a combination of dream and reality.

Several film directors, such as Méliès, Buñuel, and Bergman have explained how they were attracted to cinema through their practice of and taste for projecting shadows. The idea that cinema is a theater of shadows, is for example the basis of the work of

[51] Gilles Deleuze, *The Movement-Image,* trans. Hugh Tomlinson and Barbara Habberjam. (Minneapolis: U of Minnesota P. 1986, our adaptation).

Syberberg, for whom if we only insist on photography and motion as the specificities of cinema, that is to forget that "in the cradle of cinema, there was something else: projection and transparency."[52] This is also the basis of Raúl Ruiz's cinema, in which projected shadows often act instead of bodies, and the image reveals its complex nature.

*Projection* must be understood both as the machinery that transfers images onto the surface of a screen, and the subtle mechanism through which the viewer creates mental images. In his study of the psychology of the image, in his major work *Art and Illusion*, Gombrich noted that much of the perceptual process is due to a particular way in which visual projection functions. When we look at an image, we always perceive part of the traits that an image suggests but does not contain materially. The play of projection with the non-visible part of images, causes a link to appear between what is materially present in the image, and what it suggests to our eyes without showing it to them.

Cinema also inherited its key mechanism of *sequencing* from the techniques for exercising memory based on the image. By mobilizing the implicit aspects of images, the striking images of the first palaces of memory anticipate the off-camera in cinema. By imposing a succession that organizes the images in ordered linear sequences, the well-arranged walks in the palaces of memory prefigure cinematographic *montage*.

> Montage proceeds through repetition and halts. Repetition is not the return of something identical, it is the return as possibility of what has been. Herein resides the proximity between repetition and memory. Memory, like cinema, can transform the real into possible, and the possible into the real.[53]

[52] Joseph Von Sternberg, *Souvenirs d'un montreur d'ombres*, (Paris: Robert Laffont, 1966).
[53] Giorgio Agamben, *Image et mémoire*, (Geneva: Hoëbeke, 1998).

*The Games We Play*

In traditional games, which are as old as humanity (checkers, labyrinths, snakes and ladders, hopscotch, chess, ...), the Map of Tendre, and in mind maps, humans sketch out in symbolic representations the configuration of their relationship to the world. They ritualize and codify their itineraries: signs and allegories punctuate Perceval's route, the moves made by the king or rook on the chess board are precisely defined, the dice determine the moves in snakes and ladders, and digital networks invent new rules for the games we play every day.

The Turing Test: – Alan Turing, 1950

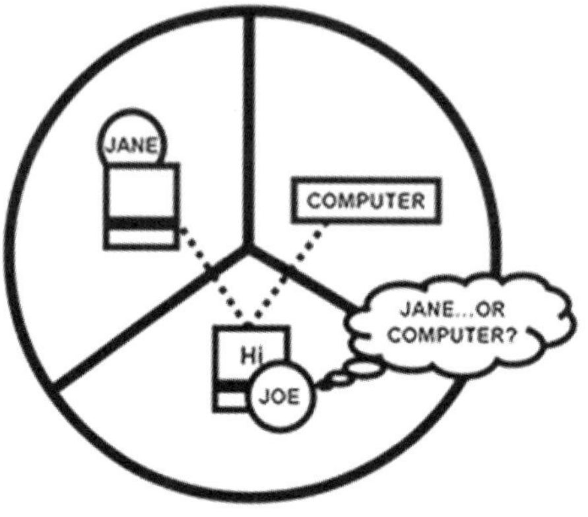


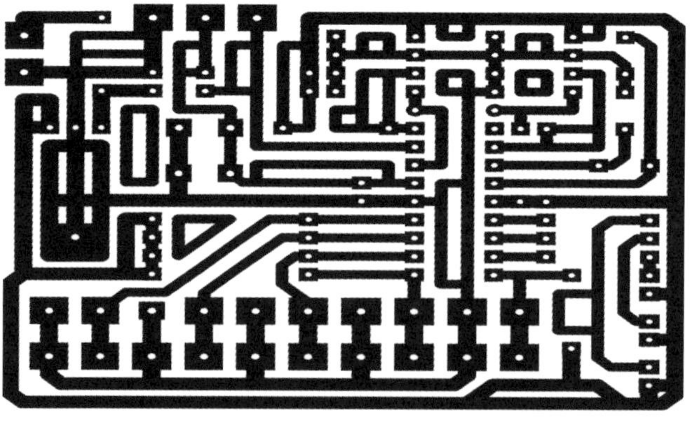

Drawing of a printed circuit in the twentieth century.

For Deleuze, images in *motion* do not only imply a time that is passing, or a chronology into which we would slip as if into a perpetual present. They also imply complex time, not only because we make our memory and expectations function in it, but also because cinema is almost capable of making us perceive time.

> It is this dynamic charge that we see very well in the photographs of Marey and Muybridge who were at the origin of cinema, images full of motion. It is a charge of this sort that Benjamin saw in what he called a dialectic image, which was for him the very basis of our historical experience. The historical experience occurs through images, and images themselves are full of history. We could consider our relationship to painting in this light: paintings are not immobile images, but rather photograms packed with motion from a film missing in our conscience. We must place them back in this film (you will have recognized Aby Warburg's project).[54]

From this perspective, cinema could be to the moving image what the palaces of memory were to the landscapes. Sitting in front of the screen, the cinema-goer — the walker who is facing chosen places — reads its language *naturally*.

[54] Giorgio Agamben, *Image et mémoire*, (Geneva: Hoëbeke, 1998), our adaption.

**M**nemosyne utilizes images and language to inscribe time in a place. It captures the fleeting sensation of the ephemeral to revivify this subjective time. Memory is not simply the superposition of images and language, rather it means going beyond them in a higher-level construction, a veritable staging process. Mnemosyne stages a scenario in a singular place, and the mental walk in this place recalls images, which mobilize language and arouse a movement of thought. Language and images ensure the transportation of the signs that make and unmake memory at every instant. Every place-image link is characterized by a third dimension—the passing of time—, which marks the order in which they appear in a scenario. Far from being photographic, memory cannot be described as a mechanical process. Images alone remember nothing, and nothing in an image is memorable without a linguistic operator. Combined with an image, language enables the movement of memory to be represented, meaning that memory is not a trace engraved in our minds, but a trajectory, tracing, scenario, or projection.

Aby Warburg's great, unfinished iconological project *Mnemosyne*, which is the closest to Camillo's Theater of Memory, shows how paradoxical it is. The creation and manipulation of images engender a culture and world the representations and visibility of which are ultimately destined to fade away progressively and enter into memory — before being lost there definitively.

> His ultimate project, *Mnemosyne*, undertaken in the 1920s, wanted to be *a history of art with no text*, a new *iconology of intervals*. It consisted of a collection of plates covered with all kinds of images, from the most scholarly to the most commonplace. By juxtaposing them, Warburg attempted to create tensions, to make appear dynamic engrams (*dynamograms)*. Clearly his approach is closer to Eisenstein and hypertext than to traditional art history.[55]

This atlas was supposed to be a gigantic condenser of all of the currents of energy in Europe, while taking shape in its phantasms (as defined by Giordano Bruno). The very name *Mnemosyne* recalls Giulio Camillo's sixteenth century Theater of Memory. Warburg wanted to interrogate this memory of *the life of images*, through various approaches including Nietzsche's eternal recurrence, Darwin's biological memory, and Freud's unconscious. By multiplying the points of view, he revealed how the image is at once evanescence (phantom) and obsession (revenant). *Mnemosyne* is the labyrinth-like expression of this process of editing, and has indeed been compared to the editing work of Jean-Luc Godard, who was greatly inspired by Warburg in the making of his *Histoire(s) du cinéma*.

### *Labyrinth, Memory, Forgetfulness*

In his movie *The Shining*, Stanley Kubrick injects into cinema the same power of manipulation given by Bruno to memory palaces. The Overlook Hotel is transformed into a potential play space by two

[55] Alain Montesse. "nT@M," seminar Ecrit-image-oral et nouvelles Technologies, Paris, Jussieu 2002.

players, the father (Jack) and his son (Danny). The game plunges dramatically into horror when the father wants to intervene in his son's play space. It is in a new play space, the hedge maze, in which a deadly chase takes place, that their competition comes to an end. For Vidal, *The Shining* represents

> an apology of magical thinking, as defined by Giordano Bruno. It is once again an itinerary linking the perversion of the fantastic genre with a kind of hermeticism, which he adored and utilized to dissimulate his subject. There is no doubt that, for Kubrick, magic as a technique for manipulating people has a contradictory relationship with power, both in terms of self-control and controlling others. It is somewhat similar to the effort involved in visualizing the invisible center of the mandala, and close to the efforts of an inner alchemy. He saw a Western-style initiatory route in the labyrinth, which is the recurring figure in *The Shining*.[56]

For Bruno, the labyrinth figures a complex itinerary with an uncertain end. Bruno's labyrinth, and the voyage into the aleatory it engenders, is thus presented as one of the figures that constitutes an interface between the mechanisms of the gardens of memory and those of contemporary arts. In both cases, the labyrinth inscribes in the landscape a cosmogony of a decentered universe, which implies new ways of gazing. The labyrinth is the trademark of the Baroque, the metaphor of suspended time, in which life itself becomes a labyrinth, in which the labyrinth appears to be an introduction towards something beyond. In the movies of Wojciech Has, *The Hourglass Sanatorium* and *The Saragossa Manuscript*, the necessarily subjective vision of what a character perceives through a window offers the occasion to enter a universe of another imaginary or oneiric dimension. As in the memory

[56] Jordi Vidal, *Traité du combat moderne -films et fictions de Stanley Kubrick*, (Paris: Allia, 2005).

palaces, it is through these openings that we move from a real space to a virtual space, which proves to be labyrinth-like and maintains a strong identity with time as it appears in dreams, phantasms and recollections. For there to be a labyrinth, we must also pass through the same places, get lost while returning from where we came. The hero of *The Saragossa Manuscript* attempts to cross the Sierra Morena desert, but is unsuccessful because he always ends up in the same place, at the deserted Venta Quemada Inn, where he discovers leftovers from a meal and spider webs, instead of the enchanted place where he had met two beautiful Muslim women.

The labyrinth is a disordered series of places that leads to a questioning of time. In the short story "Tlön, uqbar, urbis Tertius," Borges imagines a world that is only temporal, a planet on which people "conceive the universe as a series of mental processes which do not develop in space but successively in time."[57]

In all of the short stories in which he deals with the labyrinth-like nature of time, Borges explores the loss of identity engendered by it, and hints at the solution it requires to save those who err in the temporal mazes of madness. Those who continually become other, will end up one day becoming what they were. The cyclical nature of time is its ultimate secret.

The mechanism of the labyrinth is based on the implementation of an implacable dialectic linking memory and forgetfulness. Each level in the labyrinth imposes that we go beyond both the former and the latter. In "Funes the Memorius," Borges evokes the suffering of a mnemonist, Funes, who

> has such a perfect memory that he is incapable of making generalizations. He dies very young, overwhelmed by this

[57] Jorge Luis Borges, *Labyrinths: Selected Stories & Other Writings*, (New York: New Directions 1962) 7, accessed at art.yale.edu/file_columns/0000/0066/borges.pdf.

> memory that a god could have lived with, but not a man. Funes cannot forget anything. Consequently, he cannot think, because thinking requires us to make generalizations; that is, to forget. He was the solitary spectator of a multifarious, instantaneous, and nearly intolerably precise world.[58]

Memory needs forgetfulness. The ancient treatises already recommended to sometimes clean out the palaces of memory, by using for instance a snow storm. And today, computer scientists are confronted with the necessity of deleting data on a regular basis.

At the dawn of the twentieth century, the Surrealists, prolonging the experimentations in wandering of writers like Baudelaire and Rimbaud, systematized the principle of a game of wandering, which was ordered by accidental encounters in an urban landscape. All of the events lived or experienced, ranging from the insipid to the miraculous, are not only taken into consideration, but also considered to be stimulants for minds in search of any kind of excitation. In the 1950s, Guy Debord and the Situationists would invent new rules for this game of *flânerie*: "We did not seek the formula for overturning the world in books, but in wandering. Ceaselessly drifting for days on end, none resembling the one before."[59] In the Situationist drifting, strolling was no longer in phase with memory, but rather with forgetfulness. Contrary to the precise itinerary of the mnemonist or of the pilgrim, this drifting did not aim to establish a thought. Contrary to the *flânerie* of the nineteenth century, drifting is not a sign of any indulgence toward the world. Drifting can be considered as an attempt to neutralize memory and all the links uniting place and function. Situationist drifting is much more like a palace of forgetfulness than like a palace of memory. For

[58] Jorge Luis Borges, *Fictions*, (Paris, Gallimard, 1965).
[59] Guy Debord, *In girum imus nocte et consumimur igni*, trans. Ken Knabb, (2003) www.bopsecrets.org/SI/debord.films/ingirum.htm.

it is on the basis of the obliteration of our conscience of the ancient relations of necessity that new undetectable and unexpected relations can be established. The Situationists believed that the creative power of interconnecting places, images and thoughts, cannot be entrusted to any external mechanism, not even to cinema.

*Connections, Memory, and Symbolic Arrangements*

Memory is not only storage. Memory work imposes on images of the past the scrambling and recomposition inherent in a new staging process. It is always based on what is absent from the image (outside the frame) that memory weaves its networks. Above all, the arts of memory fall within the scope of fiction and the novel. Memory is a pure product of our imagination. It is therefore that which overflows the strict consignment of the real. Memory is not something deposited in a precise point of the mind, not archives, nor a gallery of portraits in which the images of the past patiently await to be summoned and reproduced in present recollections. It does not store the image perceived, nor does it duplicate it, contrary to photography, which preserves the precise trace of its object and can make an unlimited number of identical prints.

Like writing, memory is a force at work that creates connections. Memories are not dated. They are falsified by the narrative we invent with them. Any memory, even visual, is a narrative. The concept of memorization is linked to the concept of narration. Any practice linked to memorization supposes an order, and this order is first of all temporal. Time and memory are unraveled and recomposed incessantly, and in this process each of them modifies the other: memory reconstructs past time, and the time that goes by transforms our memory every day.

The invention of the printing press during the Renaissance interrupted our recourse to memory by imposing new rules on communication: the fixity of the contents (printed copies of books are identical), focus on the author (rupture with the anonymity of the scribes), the passivity of the reader (interaction with the reader became impossible). These rules generally dominated all forms of communication for three centuries—the book, theater, painting, the graphic arts, music, photography, and cinema. Today, these rules have been pulverized by digital technologies, which close the reign of Gutenberg, and put the palaces of memory back into the game of communication.

Aby Warburg was one of the first pioneers in the revival of the arts of memory,[60] who until recently was considered to be an eccentric, or as a promising art historian from Florence, who unfortunately succumbed to folly. Warburg was the eldest child, in line to inherit his family's investment bank in Hamburg. He forfeited his right to his younger brother in exchange for the promise that he would buy him all the books he ever wanted. He would acquire tens of thousands of volumes that would make up his famous library, which was moved to London in 1933 to protect it from the Nazis, and where Gombrich and Yates would subsequently work. Warburg continuously reorganized the way books were filed according to his research and in a social and historical perspective that consisted in "decomposing [his oeuvre] in such a way that would clearly highlight its material or essential heterogeneity."[61] Toward the end of his life, he would say: "When I look back on my life's journey, it appears to me that my function has been to serve the watersheds

[60] For more information on Warburg (1866 – 1923), see Philippe Alain Michaud, *Aby Warburg et l'image en mouvement,* (Paris : Macula, 1998); Georges Didi-Huberman, *L'image survivante - Histoire de l'art au temps des fantômes selon Aby Warburg*, (Paris: Editions de Minuit, 2002).

[61] Serge Trottein, «La Naissance de l'iconologie», Daniel Arasse et al., *Symboles de la Renaissance*, vol. 2 (Paris: Presses de l'École Normale Supérieure, 1982) 34.

(Wetterschhelde) of culture as a seismograph of souls."[62] He was thus the inventor of iconology, a method of analysis that decomposes the work of art by examining its conditions of production as well as the message they are likely to convey by recontextualizing them in their era. Even when travelling, he wanted to have all his books and images close at hand, so he could observe them and instantaneously establish comparisons, make analogical comparisons and symbolic arrangements, with no respect for chronologies. This *dance of books* may well have been inspired by the snake ritual of the Hopi Indians, whom he went to visit in 1895.

Warburg's *Mnemosyne Atlas* stages a sort of direct and evolving dialog with works of art, the meaning of which is permanently constructed and deconstructed through this confrontation. The juxtaposition of works creates connections, relations, and contradictions, which in turn transform the way we see these works. The tension arising from this approach disrupts what seems to be self evident, and puts our imagination to work. Order and disorder complement each other in a process that is similar to cinematographic editing. The connaisseurs dialogue with the paintings, listen to the characters, and get involved in their theater, because they play a role in it that has been prepared by painting. The mental journey does not take place in a virtual architecture, but in the organized (and disorganized) presentation of the works. This process is very close to those that characterize the arts of memory. For Warburg, the viewers of his *Mnemosyne Atlas* take the painting in the novel of which they are the heroes. This novel makes no appeal to discourse or scenario, it simply appeals to an optical process constituted by the mobility of the viewer, who looks at the paintings while strolling about; that is, while varying the

[62] Qtd. in Svetlana Boym, *Another Freedom: The Alternative History of an Idea*, (Chicago: U Chicago P): 56.

distances and points of view. Warburg's research suggests that movement is already present in the still image. In his *Salons*, Diderot had already intuited such a process by exposing a paradox, a project, and an invention. The paradox was that of movement, the invention was an optical process that manufactured variations of images, and the project was like an ironic and aloof philosophy of history. With Warburg, the mobility alluded to by Diderot overflows the limits of the perceptual sphere of painting, acquiring the tools of the illusion of movement, such as the frame, zoom, blur, tracking shot, relief, and depth of field.

### *"We should have said Mnemosyne"*

Raúl Ruiz's cinema, which appeared in the 1970s, was placed under the sign of *Mnemosyne*:

> Now I know the word: we should have said *Mnemosyne;* that is the meeting point of literature and the image, text and the image, the spoken word and the image, and the image in motion, I mean, everything that constitutes these impure arts, the audiovisual arts.[63]

This exceptional filmmaker from Chile moved to France after Pinochet's *coup d'état* in 1973, and would produce an exuberant, labyrinth-like, baroque, boundless, and hybrid œuvre, which was unquestionably marked by the arts of memory, as for instance, the movie *Three Lives and Only One Death* (1996). Raúl Ruiz short-circuits our minds, makes all the arts move towards all the other arts, jumps from theater to writing, reimplants mnemotechnical devices in the widest range of creations, going even beyond Western memory.

[53] Raúl Ruiz, Du jour au lendemain, France Culture, May 22, 1995.

> For example, the so-called *memorillas*: theatrical spies, almost always women, who would go to the performances of seventeenth-century plays in Spain in order to steal them and publish them before anyone else; they were able to remember them perfectly after attending only one show. I like to imagine they used their own faces as loci, or memory palaces, and that their grimaces and other facial expressions were the images — but certainly it must have been more complex than that. It is possible that they were able to listen to the totality of the text and superimpose it to their face en bloc, like the message transmitted by the drums in Africa: a body of messages with no syntax, immediately recognizable, like the face of a beloved being or the paella that your mother used to cook.[64]

Raúl Ruiz would push his renewal of memory palaces as far as possible, this mental walk in the image-phantasms and narrative-labyrinths, a journey marked by numerous digressions and deviations, fiction-rebuses, narrative points of view impossible to situate, verbal escapades close to the automatic writing of the Surrealists. Ruiz considers his cinema to be *poeisis*—an art of time. It is an experience of time that requires the viewer to engage in memory work via a process of reminiscence in which an intermediate state is created between the waking state and sleep, that of a time "refound." Moreover, Raúl Ruiz is delighted when viewers nod off temporarily during his movies, because every time they reawake, this creates "new paths for the imagination engendering a new coherence of the movie."[65] His movies appear then to be small machines for creating dreams and phantasms (as

[64] Raúl Ruiz, *Poetics of Cinema 1, Miscellanies*, trans. Brian Holmes, ( Paris, Éditions Dis Voir, 2005), our adaptation.

[65] Remarks made by Jean-Luc Bideau at the screening of the film *Fado majeur et mineur*, 10th Cinémaginaire Festival, Argelès sur Mer, France, May 1995.

understood in the Middle Ages), with a constant oscillation between fascination and hypnosis, and demystification and hoax. In this process, he strived to transpose into the world of cinema, the basic elements found in palaces of memory: the wandering in places, linked to images, linked to thoughts.

> The image-locus-text triad, which constitutes the corpus of techniques of classical memory, sums up in a certain sense what I mean by image. If we are able to reduce these three elements to their possible signification in cinema we obtain the following: "expressive image," "sequence" or "journey," and "implicit narration." As we can see, these three terms are linked to a single process and are inseparable.[66]

Raúl Ruiz's cinema advances via figures, which are meant to be set in memory, and are self-reflexive like a mirror; that is to say, they include the viewer within their spatiality. Viewers find themselves transported in the image, or more precisely, with it. At the same time, these images exclude the viewer, in the permanent challenge of the codes linked to the credibility of images. This subtle game of inclusion-exclusion incites the viewers to let themselves be carried away by the images at any time, and at the same time to analyze them from a distance. Other images from other movies are sometimes linked to these figures. In this case, links are made through references and connivance, identification, and the recognition of forms and themes.

With Raúl Ruiz, cinema is no longer only images, but above all a question of time. The long tradition that links the arts of memory and cinema suddenly appears to be natural and essential. This hypothesis is no longer merely due to point of view, a sort of haphazard construction in hindsight of an ancestor of cinema. The

[66] Raúl Ruiz, *Poetics of Cinema 2*, Trans. Carlos Morreo (Paris: Éditions Dis Voir, 2005), our adaptation.

intuitions concerning mental walking, image-phantasms, putting into motion still images, image-texts or projections, as the essential elements that constitute cinema, now become self-evident, and we can no longer underestimate them. This revelation produces the same effect as when I discovered, suddenly late in life, that the distinctive sign of Bordeaux wines, is this slight taste of sweet pepper, which I had never identified as such, and will never be able to forget. And I wonder why something so obvious had not affected me much earlier! With Raúl Ruiz, cinema is indeed at the end of that improbable chain, which has transmitted, link by link, since the first palaces of memory, a certain way of thinking in images. There is no longer a missing link, and if a link proves to be inexistent or too weak, Raúl Ruiz always has some parallel link in reserve to re-establish the transmission.

## VIRTUAL LANDSCAPES

While, in terms of putting information into memory, the passage from mnemotechnical devices to audiovisual and then digital media has involved transformations in our vision of the world, in reality there has not been a true break. The memory machine has always developed like an image-producing machine or a machine for thinking in images. Beyond the changes in media, this process entails a journey by the subject through the labyrinth of their architecture, because the arts of memory condition the changing status of images as well as places. As for the images, the places range from the private architecture of each individual to shared public buildings.

From memory palaces to virtual landscapes, it has always been a matter of mentally walking through imaginary landscapes. However, the utopia of a world in the head has become a collective utopia. As if, by opening up this path, the world were attempting to inscribe the movement of a fourth dimension in two-dimensional space. Today, this field of action enjoys new prospects, since humanity is quite close to being able to create life from scratch. The boundary between the real and the virtual has become so porous that the real might soon appear as something virtual transformed into matter, and the body as something virtual transformed into an organism. The dream of *a world in the head* might soon become that of *a world in the body*. Yet, whether we are considering information or living things, networking

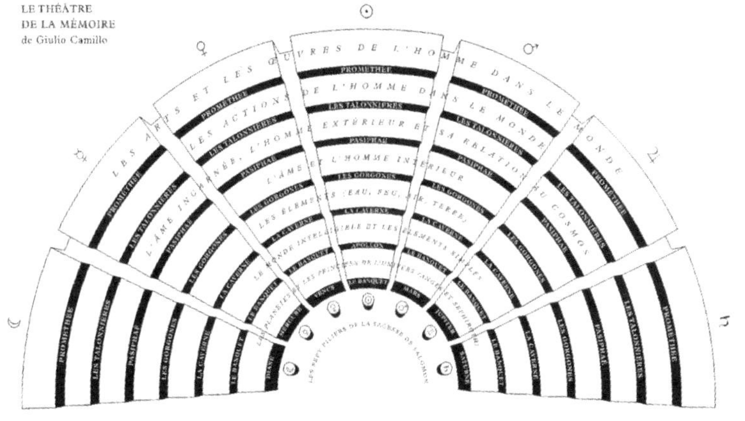


The Theater of Memory – Giulio Camillo sixteenth century

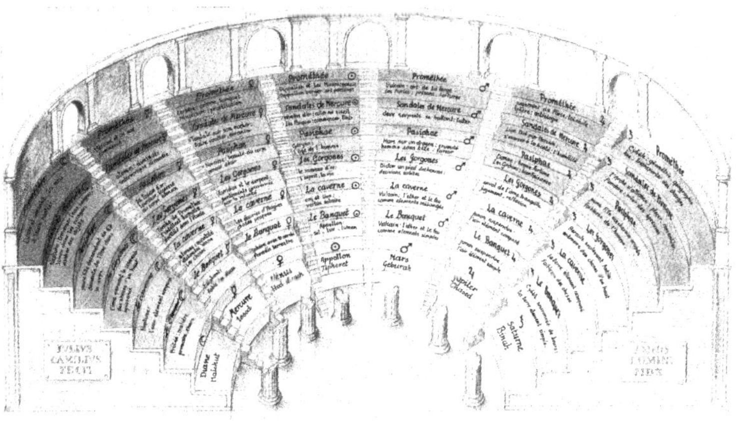

*Theater of Memory / Theater of the World*

The countless loci created by the arts of memory for over 2500 years are both concrete and yet rather fluid.

They have taken on the forms of palaces of memory, gardens of knowledge, sun or cosmic cities, sacred mounts, theaters of the world, magic lanterns, cinematographic theaters, and now virtual theaters-- these new spaces of representation, with their icons, windows, portals, links and hypertexts. Virtuality, along with digitization, hypertext, tree diagrams, and interactivity are being combined in new forms of creation.

generally emphasizes the container, the network itself, with the risk of not questioning the content, and moving toward the pure optimization of data and bodies. It is a major issue for humanity today to avoid this kind of instrumentalization.

Over the centuries, the age-old language-image link gradually strengthened until the Middle Ages, before weakening from the Renaissance to the twentieth century after the invention of the printing press, and then being revived today because of the new possibilities afforded by audiovisual applications and multimedia. The status of images has followed the same paradigm shift, so that we now consider the image not as the visible but as the visual, not as a world of shapes, but as a concretion of time, obligating, according to Georges Didi-Huberman, art history to turn back into an art of history, an art of memory:

> When we look at an image, no matter how ancient, the present never ceases to be reconfigured as long as the dispossession of the gaze has not entirely given way to the vain complacency of the specialist. When we look at an image – as recent or contemporary as it may be – the past never ceases to be reconfigured, since this image only becomes thinkable in a construction of memory (…) we are the fragile element facing it, the passing element, while it is the element of the future, the one that will endure.[67]

### *Expanded Cinema, Digital Images, and Immemory*

In spite of being occulted for three centuries, and undoubtedly because of the tenacity of rare philosophers such as Leibniz and Vico, the arts of memory reappeared at the end of the nineteenth

[67] Georges Didi-Huberman. *Before Time*. 2008 p. 32 (our adaptation of text at: library.tulane.edu/.../83cf6254c0af98be169121d9babb2f08.pdf

century behind a mask in cinema and psychoanalysis, and increasingly openly in the audiovisual arts of the twentieth century. Dziga Vertov was one of the first directors who laid the foundations of modern cinema. By inventing cine-eye, he advanced the idea of capturing *improvised life*, definitively doing away with the passive recording of images. The images from real life must be refigured, and Vertov would devote all the resources of emerging cinema to this recreation. "Such that, through agitations, shreds and frictions, the basic fragments of the movie are placed in a singular arrangement; this was a new system that drew on the order of the fragments as much as on the disorder of their relations; an order *inscribed as possibility*, an order that did not exist anywhere as a whole, one aiming to unveil or change the world."[68] Vertov invented montage, and his cine-eye-ear is oddly reminiscent of Simonides's invention of poetry composed for the *eye-ear* twenty-five centuries earlier. According to Simonides, the word is the image of reality, painting is silent poetry, and poetry is painting that speaks. Vertov's cine-eye-ear finally gave birth to a poetry that moves and images that speak.

In the mid-twentieth century, anticipating the mutations in cinema and its practices, filmmakers attempted to free themselves from the constraints of classical cinema. *Expanded cinema* is the term used to designate the innovations that the development of new audiovisual techniques permitted. Expanded cinema practitioners included those engaging in experimental cinema, whose common goal was to go beyond their medium and the usual constraints of disseminating movies, using sometimes multiple projections. In this context, the movie is considered to be a performance or an installation— cinema that is truly alive.

Expanded cinema abolishes the boundaries between the different means of expression by employing elements other

[68] Guy Chapoulie, «L'autre séparation,» *Entrelacs 5*, Nov. 2005.

> than film: painting (Jeff Keen painting the screen during the projection), video (George Saxon), and even photography (pictures developing in *Exposed* by Steve Farrer), and going as far as redefining the geography of the screening room (projections on two screens on opposite walls in *Light Music* by Liz Rhodes).[69]

Dominique Noguez describes expanded cinema as "any show that goes beyond or modifies the cinematographic ritual." Expanded cinema has now been dissolved in the infinite variations of the image in motion, from experimental cinema to video-art, multimedia installations, and VJ sets.

It is certainly in the digital arts that we must look for the most contemporary resurgence of new memory palaces. This relationship between the arts of memory and the on-line and off-line deployment of multimedia can be seen in the attempts to map cyberspace, to make a system of places from all of its sites, to reproduce in increasingly small chips the labyrinth-like structure of mnemonic devices.

The same procedure can be found in the production of computer generated images, which are entirely conceived through programming and have no referent in the real world. Such images have become digital instead of analogical creations. With photography, the image remains a tangible object because of the paper medium. With cinema, it became an ephemeral luminous projection on the screen (which is not the image), but the underlying photogram remains an object. The digital image fully dematerializes the image, which is transformed into an electronic signal, scanned, read on the screen, transmitted by wires or waves, compressed and stored on a disk, with no loss of information, and still able to be corrected and transformed with software. Digital sound follows the same path towards being dematerialized using new technologies—

[69] "Cinéma différent," *Art Press International* 18 (May 1978).

the utilization of the computer makes it possible to create infinitely variable sounds and acoustic components. Finally, in the world of computing, numerous examples hint at the underlying influence of the tradition of the arts of memory, such as the ergonomic Apple operating system, the proliferation of geolocation applications, and semantic norms on Internet. The digital era no longer deals with imaginary objects distributed in invented architectures, but computer data (files, interactive sites, data banks) to which computer networks ensure a connection.

Robert Kramer, a tireless explorer of planet earth, and a great documentary filmmaker, apprehends the new creative possibilities opened up by new technologies as follows:

> Chris Marker's cinema is the one I am interested in that deals with the problematic of the real. More specifically, his work in *The Last Bolshevik,* not necessarily what he did in *Level Five*. Or perhaps in his minimalistic relations with new technology, such as the red beam that helps us to discover old documents. Materialization from Marker's point of view: the introduction of technology that can help create a real new language and renew it.[70]

In his 1997 movie *Immemory,* Marker puts interactivity at the service of a labyrinth-like exploration of culture, memory, and imagination:

> My working hypothesis was that any rather long memory is more structured than it might seem to be. That the photos taken apparently by chance, the postcards chosen according to how we feel at a given moment, as of a certain threshold begin to sketch out an itinerary, to map the imaginary country extending within us. By working my way

[70] *Cinémaginaire* 11 (May 2001).

> through it systematically, I was sure I would discover that the apparent disorder of my imagery was hiding a *map*, like in a pirate story.[71]

Marker explicitly places contemporary ditigal arts in the tradition of the arts of memory:

> The compass I used is based on points of reference quite far back in history. Curiously, it is not the immediate past that offers us models for what could be computer navigation on the theme of memory. It is overly dominated by the arrogance of the classical narrative and the positivism of biology. The art of memory is on the contrary a very ancient discipline, which was progressively forgotten (unbelievably!) just as the divorce was taking place between physiology and psychology. In other words, when I proposed to transfer the regions of memory in geographic rather than historical terms; without knowing it, I was re-establishing a link with a conception familiar to some thinkers in the seventeenth century, but completely foreign to those of the twentieth.[72]

We circulate in Marker's universe as if we were in a building, moving from one room to another through doors and staircases—each of the rooms has its functions and atmospheres, which reflect and modify the people living there. Chance and subjectivity preside over the itinerary, and the cat is the guiding figure orienting the tree diagrams towards hypertext and hyperimages. Marker's multimedia writing creates the fragments of a discourse and the space of a language, the tool for representing the world and memory. This language is situated between architecture and cinema, and provides a kinetic vision of the places built. It offers the arts of memory an unexpected renaissance.

[71] *www.instantsvideo.com/archives/pmb/opac_css/index.php?lvl=notice_display&id=62*
[72] *www.derives.tv/Immemory*

*Virtual Theaters and Hypertextual Narratives*

Something virtual does not exist concretely, but potentially. The virtual constitutes a rupture with respect to the idea that art is a representation of reality: it does not purport to be an imitation or an artifice, rather it aims to replace the real itself. In the interactive processes between users and the system, the space simulated does not correspond to any existing space, the time simulated remains outside of any present, past or future, with no end or origin. But while in the perception of a real being, it is the movement of this real being that determines the point of view of the visible world, here it is the objects of this visible world that begin moving in the virtual gaze of an immobile observer.

Ted Nelson invented the word *hypertext* in 1965, which he conceived to be first of all literary media, while computing was for him a sub-branch of cinema. One idea obsessed him—that of bringing together nearly all of the literary works from all the heretofore published genres. Via the network, readers would have access to the texts that interested them, and could link the texts between themselves as they saw fit. Openings would be possible towards all kinds of documents. The corpus could evolve and extend continuously. New documents would make it possible to add links and itineraries infinitely. All digitizable data can now be added to these resource texts, including images, sounds, music, maps, and images in motion. Every piece of data used marks a station in the hypertextual journey. Nelson's project is the dream of an infinite library, in which books refer to other books, and the library never stops expanding. This hypertextual exploration irresistibly recalls the metaphor of the library employed by Borges in the "Library of Babel." It also makes us think of the inventions of Ramon Llull, for whom the links between ideas and images helped to structure and organize knowledge. These techniques, which were used in medieval illuminations, were abandoned when the printing press was invented, but are being revived today in the system of links on which hypertext is based. The difference with respect to the artificial memory devised by the arts of memory, is that hypertext constitutes a sort of external expansion of human memory, which increases its possibilities infinitely, whereas the ancient arts of memory were attempting, on the contrary, to make the entire universe–and our knowledge of it–enter our minds.

What the arts of memory had first intuited—that there is time in images—is now central to the digital arts. Images in motion designate practices more than images. Images have become active, attracting the viewer's gaze, as Kafka had already observed: "the gaze does not take possession of images, it is images that take possession of the gaze." Somewhere between a cinema in which viewers are inextricably caught up in the flow of images, and the pure fiction an individual can create freely, contemporary art calls for the active participation of the viewer.

In *Eavesdrop* (Australia 2004) by David Pledger and Jeffrey Shaw, viewers sit at the center of the panoramic projection experience. They can control the movement of the camera with a dashboard, and by reframing the scene they can observe characters and listen to conversations. Among the characters present, a couple watches the viewers and speaks about them. The viewing position is staged, and the set-up gives the illusion of an inversion, with the characters in the movie watching the viewers as if they were part of the scene.

The core themes of *Remake* (Pierre Huyghe 1995) are cinema (conceived as a reserve of images and stories), spatial-temporal reversibility, and the close but ambiguous relationship between the real and fiction. For Huyghe, fiction appears in the shadows of reality, which are zones we are constantly inventing, as if we wanted to fill in the holes in reality. His approach is a deliberate attempt to grasp the real. *Remake* is a 100-minute remake of Alfred Hitchcock's movie *Rear Window*. It is filmed in an amateurish way, and we can see the difficulties facing the actors as well as the camera operators. In his undertaking, Huyghe reveals the process through which a piece of fiction is created. In these remakes, he exploits the notion of play to escape from traditional narrative structures, distort and extend them beyond their own limits. Through the effects of *mise en abyme*, a remake enacts a critique of the narrative system structuring a movie of which it is nonetheless a remake.

The open crates that constitute the work by Sarkis entitled *The Treasure Chest of Mnemosyne* (1996) are a heartfelt tribute to Aby Warburg. For Sarkis, our memory of artistic works does not really function in terms of content, style or intention, as museology and art history suppose; nor only on the level of free association as the Surrealists imagined. Sarkis's work continues the works of Warburg and Benjamin, who perceive human history (and therefore art history) as a reserve of potential energy, which oscillates between the domination of the present and the recourse to reason by calling on historical time. For the artist, this possible energy, which is most often unused or falsified, hangs on a thread—that of the critical conscience. Time is no longer linear on this thread. It can be twisted and turned continuously, which enables forms to be created and reactivated, while taking action. This thread links the personal memory of artists to world history. In its fragility, this thread is the very matter of Sarkis's art.

*The Holbein Project* (1998–2000) by Catherine Beaugrand, oscillates between a house of mirrors and an optics laboratory. It evokes the work on perspective of the Renaissance painter Hans Holbein the Younger, and in particular his famous painting *The Ambassadors* (1533). Glass architecture, a mathematical-theoretical diamond, this labyrinth of transparent screens, placed on or rising up from a metal base, is in fact the exact three-dimensional projection of the multiple points of view in the painting. Beaugrand's installation is nonetheless diametrically opposed to the geometric optics developed during the Renaissance, with the gazing point contributing to the ambiguity in exactly the same way as in Lacan. Penetrating then moving within this laboratory, the viewer actively participates in multiplying the visual and the virtual projections, the vanishing lines, partitions, and fields. *The* Ambassadors is generally noticed by art historians and psychoanalysts for its anamorphic skull in the foreground. The techniques of representation chosen by the painter seem to have an overall coherence, while many of the objects represented are depicted from a single point of view—each object is represented from its own point of view. The reality effect is thus condensed in objects, but these are objects the form of which seems to have been entirely subordinated to questions of seeing. Beaugrand's goal, five centuries after Holbein, is indeed to question our means of representation, and to suggest that each of us should create our own point of view.

### *Interactivity and Collective Intelligence*

Interactivity is one of the major contributions made by new technologies. It is a function created by them, which enables real time reciprocal actions in a dialogic mode, a back-and-forth process between humans and machines. Digital interactivity is based on the principle of the universal commutability of data in the form of matrixes of numbers. Interactivity was already one of the essential

*Links and Community*

With the creation of links, the notion of network (the web) is progressively replacing that of structure, which was inherited from the human sciences and mathematics of the nineteenth and twentieth centuries.
The term networks refers to the organic,
the living (tissue),
and the technical (weaving). It figures a fluid, flexible, tree-like organization, created by the computer,
at both the personal and planetary levels.
The web and its interactive practices provide new possibilities for reinventing Bruno's expanding universe,
this sphere with no circumference the center of which is everywhere.

*Utopia,* Thomas More 1516.

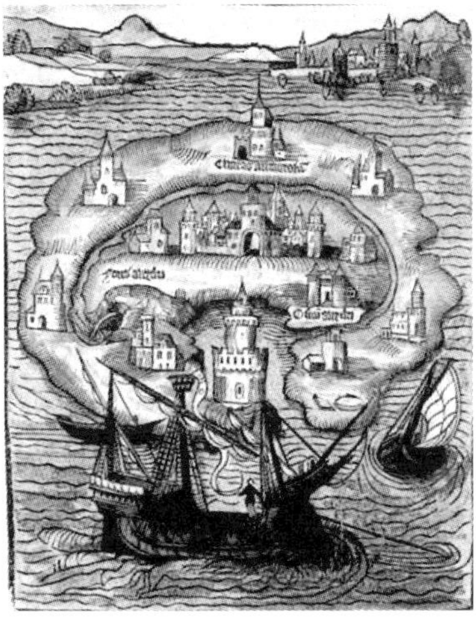

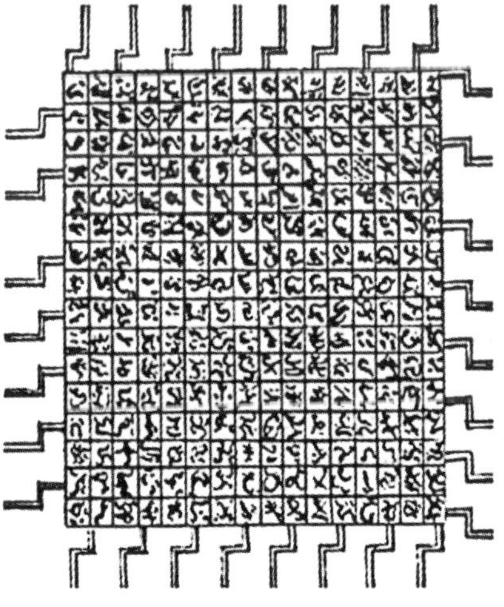

*Literary Engine* –Literary generator using chance and permutations – Jonathan Swift 1735

mechanisms in Camillo's Theater of Memory, as a principle of connections between knowledge and the symbolic images placed in a set of well-ordered boxes. Paradoxically, this problematic of links, central to the question of art today, is closely akin to the one Bruno asked defiantly in the sixteenth century. Bruno considered the celestial globe to be a theater of which he could carefully open the boxes one at a time. In this process, he transformed an infinite space into an arena with its own dynamics. Images are formed, reflecting on the one hand the desire to grasp the expression of life, and on the other, the need to take distance from immediacy and construct a representation of it. Seeing and representing are at the two opposite ends of an ellipsis, of which the intermediate space, the link, is to be ensured by the work of art. Art is to some extent the link between these two extremities. This search for a link between absolute science and absolute poetry cost Bruno his life. The link of all links, Cupid's link according to Bruno, the one Marsilio Ficino was already calling true magic, is the one that transforms power into acts, and acts into power. It is this force of the link that is being reborn today through the interactivity of digital processes. This force is no longer the instrument of a small number of initiated individuals, rather it is that of the entire human community, enabling us to access all the knowledge we put in common, develop, and ultimately control. It is no longer the artificial memory of a few people, but a collective intelligence, according to the expression of Pierre Lévy, which has been pushing humanity to become the subject of its own inquiry.

Only the person who had conceived the mental images of the ancient memory palaces could walk in them. This space could not be shared. On the contrary, according to Rieusset-Lemarié:

> The materialization of this virtual architecture on external media, allows others to view it, or even to stroll in it in a data costume. In interactive virtual reality, we can create an imaginary urban landscape, which is no longer a completely mental landscape. We can technologically devise password protected computer assisted memory palaces. In this process, we can sketch out the contours of not only an imaginary urban landscape but of a veritable virtual city.[73]

It is in this interactive space that the memory palaces can reemerge today, with the infinite possibilities opened by a hypertextual structure. In interactive hypertext, we can all invent our own personal itineraries, moving from one step to the next by simply clicking. The private places of the ancient memory palaces can become public labyrinths, in which the person walking advances from one image to another, each new place opening up a passage to others. These new places, which are accessible to everyone, but by means of which each person can create a singular itinerary, embody a veritable paradigm shift. The creation, utilization, sharing, and development of the arts of memory now entail a collective undertaking. This new human activity also shakes up the history of representation in another way: undermining several centuries of supremacy of one-point perspective and two-dimensional representations, the three-dimensional universe of virtual realities re-establishes links with the mental architectures of the first memory palaces. “Virtual architecture would be for this reason the ideal mnemotechnical structure, because it preserves the three-dimensional nature of architecture while conferring upon it the purely virtual nature of the image, which enables the symbolic inscription and no longer only a material trace of memory to be strengthened.”[74]

[73] Isabelle Riusset-Lemarié. «Des palais de mémoire aux paysages virtuels,» *Les enjeux du paysage*, (Brussels: Ousia, 1997).
[74] Rieusset-Lemarié.

Finally, this art, which inextricably binds language and the image while renewing the art of montage and ellipses, invents experimentations in which representation becomes self-referential. These new memory palaces are places in which we can experiment with what Gonzalez-Fœrster has called *art sensations*.

In his video trilogy *The Middle Passage / Cayenne / The Edge of the World* (2006), Mathieu K. Abonnec attempts to delineate the ways in which historical events take on a collective reality and take shape in the memory and unconscious of everyone. One of these ways is through storytelling, in which fictive representation tends to replace eye-witness accounts of the real event. Often, it even acquires the value of a document, able to produce in turn a new fiction, until the first eye-witness accounts have been lost. His trilogy was made by juxtaposing images taken from Hollywood films. These images are defective or blurry because they were recorded with a video recorder. It is mainly images of partially visible landscapes. In the movies from which these images were taken, the landscapes are not recognizable—one image is like any other, one forest or city like any other. Just as our memory, the landscape is broken up, and immersion impossible.

With *Talk Show* (2009), Omer Fast continues his critical investigations of mass media by exploring the facets of a personal narrative that has been altered by different narrators. This personal narrative is that of Lisa Ramaci, whose husband, a journalist, was killed in Iraq because he helped a young translator escape from the country. She tells this story first, thus beginning a loop. Six interpretations of it are then given to a fake audience at a television studio, as in the children's game the broken telephone. For one hour, the narrative is modified and struggles to develop in different ways, and the initial meaning of the story is transformed even more. Yet, is it not the same for the news we are told every day? What deformations has it undergone? Are we informed about the real or about fiction? Such are the questions raised in the work of Fast.

Not only artists are taking advantage of the tremendous possibilities offered by the re-emerging arts of memory. Today, with the Internet, systems devised two thousand years ago are developing in a wide range of shapes and forms that go far beyond the techniques imagined by the mnemonists of Antiquity. However, the same basic principles are being utilized: ordering, repetitive itineraries, and image-language links. One example is the mind map invented in 1971 by the British psychologist Tony Buzan, who proposed to represent visually the unfolding of a thought or the pathway of its elaboration. Today, mind maps are everywhere on the Internet, inspire training modules, and are central to learning pedagogies. Another example are flash cards, which are cards based on drawings that help people to memorize a large number of different pieces of information. These flash cards can now be generated by on-line applications or smartphones. More generally speaking, numerous ways of data visualization have appeared with the help of new technologies, which are enabling us to present data in scenario form, to assemble images, figures, and texts to create links between data that seem to have nothing in common, and also to create a more attractive link with the audience. The core issue is to create a collective memory, a kind of interactive encyclopedia, which informs everyone and which is in turn enriched by each person—a cooperative encyclopedia, produced by internauts—, horizontal knowledge that is constantly expanding and that questions the authority of knowledge approved by a hierarchy or official knowledge. A great deal of energy has been mobilized in recent years to keep this artificial memory outside of the system of

Logo of Wikipedia - *the free encyclopedia*

commercial exchanges, and is embodied in freeware, creative commons licenses, and mutualized collaborative works like Wikipedia.

On the road that leads from the memory palaces to the most recent tree diagrams and interactive systems, it is not as much the visual nature of memory that is at stake, as our being confronted with an unexpected conclusion: memory can only be *artificial!* As if the movement of memory, which purports to counter the ravages of time, were feeding on the irrepressible desire for organization and reproduction, which if surprising, is nevertheless quite effective for braking our slide down the natural slope of disorder. As if life itself did not know how to fight against entropy except by admitting that it is itself *artificial!* As if the very principle of memory were the suspension of the semantic links attached to words and images. As if representation could only attain its goal by freeing itself from these links and becoming self-referential. As if a link superior to representation could emerge from using artifice effectively.

## ON THE ROAD! A PROVISIONAL EPILOG...

In my wanderings through the arts of memory, I have attempted to follow the fleeting traces left behind by the explorations of major figures such as Simonides, Lucretius, Ramon Llull, Pieter Aertsen, Masacio, Giulio Camillo, Gian Paolo Lomazzo, Giordano Bruno, Leibniz, Athanasius Kircher, Aby Warburg, Benjamin, Chris Marker and Raúl Ruiz. I placed all these traces on my editing table, and attempted to find links between the various practices of the arts of memory that are scattered over time and space. I tried to find continuity in the arts of memory during the periods in which they seem to have been neglected, and I have also attempted to broaden the scope of my research to the rest of the world, because most studies only focus on Europe. I have sketched out a continuous chain from Ancient Greece to the present day, and suggested possible answers where there were missing links. In the places where the chain seemed to break, there always seemed to be a person, place, image or invention to reestablish a link—a bit like biologists facing the enormous task of sequencing the human genome—that other biological memory. I was sometimes struck by vertigo while travelling along the road that links the ancient arts of memory to the contemporary world: such a long road with so many forks, so many false leads, entire sections overgrown by scrub, collapsed bridges, no precise maps, few people along the road to point me in the right direction.

On the road, the image started thinking, the text started seeing, the contemporary arts are located at the very intersection of these thinking images and seeing texts, in the long tradition of the arts of the invisible. Making our way, we can remake the world. Moreover, *making our way* can also mean *caminando* or *travelling*. I imagined a sort of global memory palace, that mobile memory and that immobile journey, the passage created between life and the representation of life, that fluidity of metamorphoses and tracking shots. The tracking shot is the very figure of images in motion, which inscribe time into space. By wandering around, we inscribe ourselves into the landscape. Through a tracking shot, the landscape is inscribed in the viewer. This itinerary leads us from one site to another down random paths. Each site arouses a thought. Each thought opens up onto a landscape, which opens the path toward a new site.

Borges, whose works certainly represent the tip of a palace-of-memory iceberg, continually highlighted the efforts of those who contributed to transmitting and enriching the ancient arts of memory:

> Toward the end of the thirteenth century, Ramón Llull (Raimundo Lulio or Raymond Lully) invented the thinking machine. Four hundred years later, Athanasius Kircher, his reader and commentator, invented the magic lantern. The first invention is recorded in a work entitled *Ars Magna Generalis*; the second, in an equally inaccessible opus called *Ars Magna Lucis et Umbrae*. The names of both inventions are generous. In reality, in mere lucid reality, the magic lantern is not magical, nor is the mechanism devised by Ramón Llull capable of thinking a single thought, however rudimentary or fallacious. To put it another way: measured against its objective, judged

> by its inventor's illustrious goal, the thinking machine does not work. For us, that fact is of secondary importance. The perpetual motion machines depicted in sketches that confer their mystery upon the pages of the most effusive encyclopedias don't work either, nor do the metaphysical and theological theories that customarily declare who we are and what manner of thing the world is. Their public and well-known futility does not diminish their interest. This may (I believe) also be the case with the useless thinking machine [...] This motionless diagram, with its nine capital letters distributed among nine compartments and linked by a star and some polygons, is already a thinking machine.[75]

The history of the various ways in which we have represented the world is brimming with inventions sketched out then abandoned, of cleverly manufactured illusions and developments that ran up against their own limits. This permanent struggle of *invenzioni* and *inganni* (creations and traps) at play in the Gardens of Bomarzo, can at any moment create an opening or instead close upon itself — and this shift can be long lasting or ephemeral. Artistic creation is a garden of bifurcating paths. Until the sixteenth century and even beyond, people were condemned to death for engaging in freethinking, which could only be transmitted secretly. We can follow freedom along its enigmatic tracks, which are completely invisible for traditional historiography. After being burned at the stake during the Inquisition, Giordano Bruno was long erased from history. The authentic sources concerning his life and his struggles were often destroyed, and we hardly knew about anything other than the tales of the very people who denounced, defamed or even executed him. Now that his writings are finally being disseminated again, Bruno astonishes us by the modernity of his engagement in the world of links

[75] Jorge Luis Borges, Selected Non-Fictions, ed. Eliot Weinberger. trans. Esther Allen, Suzanne Jill Levine and Eliot Weinberger, (New York: Penguin, 1999).

and images. His philosophy is also modern in its obstinate desire to inextricably combine magic and science, science and creativity, and our experience of the real and imagination: "Linking the mystical and cosmological geometry of Ramon Llull to the architecture and images of Giulio Camillo, Giordano Bruno harnessed the inner world of imagination to the stars and reproduced the celestial world within human beings."[76] By reinfusing life into the philosophy of Giordano Bruno, the digital arts have rediscovered the ancient conception of art as the result of a magic process, and rekindled the ancient vocation of Mnemosyne—the hidden dream of a world transformed through the combined forces of memory, poetry, and action.

At the end of this long stroll in the palaces of memory, how can I continue my tapestry of images and language? As in the *xenia*, the weaving process distances nature to render it as a still life, which is more alive nonetheless than the natural objects that have already disappeared. Something happens in this two-way movement. For the real is no longer exactly the same when it has been rendered—it becomes doubled, reinforced by fiction. Make something artificial and add a taste of nature, such is the secret of the powerful alchemy alluded to by Degas, which emerges from the uncertain forms of the arts of memory. Magic and images have always been the product of the same miracle. Any formal conclusion would distance us from these powerful attractions and these creative wanderings. In the digital age, visual thought and imagination can certainly be placed in the category of complex systems, for which the number and wide range of determiners renders impossible any complete definition, because in complex systems, the whole always greatly surpasses the sum of its parts.

[76] Jean-Michel Maulpoix, *L'Art de la Mémoire*, *www.maulpoix.ne*t.

The path through the arts of memory is certainly not the only one leading here, nor even the most direct one. But for those who take this road, the view is stunning and the vista points change continuously. This crest trail allows us to see that there is a continual revolution in the thought-image relationship. From the palaces of memory to the most recent interactive processes, images in motion maintain this agitation, are troublemakers, successively stripping the bride bare and her bachelors, even. We have been able to think in images ever since Mnemosyne started nourishing the arts with which we represent and reflect upon the world. The arts of memory introduced an exercise of thinking as art, which made knowledge evolve from a state in which it was necessary to "learn thoughts" to one in which we "learn to think". Today, this *Ars Magna* imagined by Ramon Llull, which was raised to the rank of a link by Giordano Bruno, has become a major objective of Internet—linking human beings, and through their interactions developing collective intelligence. These arts of memory have become fully meaningful today as a way of apprehending the emergence of a digital thought process, at the dawn of a new Copernican Revolution.

At the end of *The Dream of Poliphilus*, we learn that all of this is but a dream. But what a dream! Hegel had sensed that humans were already weary shortly before realizing that they really are. I love the idea according to which humans – as imagined by Giordano Bruno – dream of putting their images in motion, just before putting their dreams into action.

> This vault of heaven beneath which we stand bewildered,
> We know to be a sort of magic-lantern:
> Know thou that the sun is the flame and the universe is the lamp,
> We are like figures that revolve in it.[77]

[77] Omar Khayyam, *The Sufistic Quatrains of Omar Khayyam.* trans. Edward Fitzgerald, Edward Henry Whinfield, and J. B. Nicolas, *www.gutenberg.org/files/38511/38511-h/38511-h.htm.*

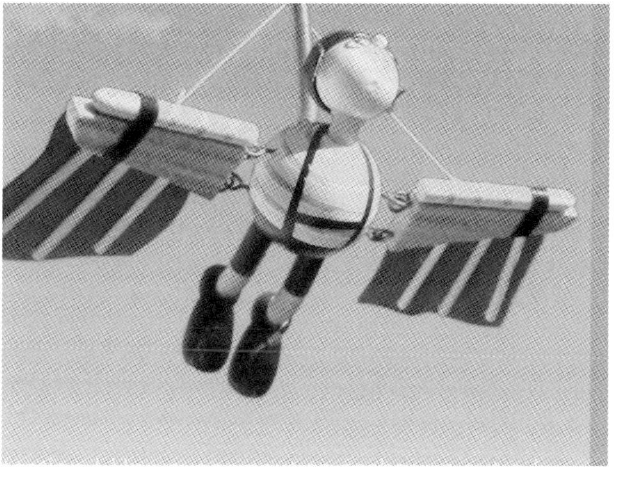

Detail of the poster of the movie Urbi et Orbi by François Boutonnet, 2007.
Film at the origins of Boutonnet's reflections on the Theater of Memory.

## BIBLIOGRAPHY


Agamben, Giorgio. Image et mémoire. Geneva: Hoëbeke, 1998.

Alberti, Leon Battista. De Pictura. 1435.

Bardini, Thierry. « Les liens de Giordano Bruno : magie, arts et sciences à l'heure du nexus. » Inter : art actuel. 97 (2007) 20-26. id.erudit.org/iderudit/45642ac.

Benjamin, Walter. The Work of Art in the Age of Mechanical Reproduction. Trans. Harry Zohn. Paris, New York: Schocken/Random House, 1969.

—-. Paris, Capital of the Nineteenth Century – The Arcades Project. Paris, New York: Belknap Press, 2002.

Bolzoni, Lina. "The Play of Images: the Art of Memory from Its Origins to the Seicento." The Enchanted Loom: Chapters in the History of Neuroscience. Oxford: Oxford UP, 1991.

—-. The Gallery of Memory: Literary and Iconographic Models in the Ages of the Printing Press. Toronto: U Toronto P, 2001.

Bomsel, Olivier and Jean-Charles Blais. «L'apparition du DVD. » History and Economy of Digitization Seminar. Cerna Ecole des Mines, EHESS, 2004.

Borges, Jorge Luis. "Tlön, Uqbar, Orbis Tertius." Labyrinths: Selected Stories & Other Writings. New York: New Directions, 1962 7, accessed at art.yale.edu/file_columns/0000/0066/borge.pdf.

—-. Fictions. Paris: Gallimard, 1965.

—-. Selected Non-Fictions, ed. Eliot Weinberger. trans. Esther Allen, Suzanne Jill Levine and Eliot Weinberger. New York: Penguin, 1999.

Boym, Svetlana. Another Freedom: The Alternative History of an Idea. Chicago: U Chicago P, 2010.

Bruno, Giordano De Umbris Idearum: On the Shadow of Ideas. Paris: 1582. Trans. Scott Gosnell.

—- Articuli Adversus Mathematicos, Prague, 1588. Stuttgart-Bad Cannstatt Frommann, 1962.

—-. Cause, Principle and Unity And Essays on Magic. Trans. Robert De Lucca. Cambridge: Cambridge UP, 1998. Trans. of De Magia, c. 1590.

Calvino, Italo. Invisible Cities. trans. William Weaver. Orlando: Harcourt Brace, 1974.

Camillo, Giulio. Le Théâtre de la Mémoire. Trans. Eva Cantavenera and Bertrand Schefer. Paris: Ed. Allia, 2001.

Cassin, Barbara. L'effet sophistique. Paris: Gallimard, 1995.

Cellarius, Andreas. Harmonia Macrocosmica, 1660.

Cesarano, Giorgio. Manuale di sopravivvenza. Bari: Dedalo, 1974.

Chapouillie, Guy. "L'autre séparation," Entrelacs 5 (Nov. 2005).

Cicero, De Oratore.Trans. Edward William Sutton. London: W.Heinemann; Cambridge: Harvard UP, 1967. www.laits.utexas.edu/memoria/Cicero.html.

Couliano, Ioan Peter. Eros and Magic in the Renaissance. Trans. Margaret Cook. Chicago: University of Chicago Press, 1987.

Courant, Gérard. «Cinéma différent.» Art Press International 18, May 1978.

Debord, Guy. In girum imus nocte et consumimur igni. Trans. Ken Knabb, 2003. www.bopsecrets.org/SI/debord.films/ingirum.htm

Deleuze, Gilles. The Movement-Image. Trans. Hugh Tomlinson and Barbara Habberjam. Minneapolis: U of Minnesota P, 1986.

—-. The Fold: Leibniz and the Baroque. Trans. Tom Conley. New York: Continuum, 2006.

de Mandiargues, André Pieyre. Les Monstres de Bomarzo. Paris: Grasset, 1957.

Detambel, Régine. « L'art de la mémoire, » www.detambel.com/f/index.php?sp=liv&livre_id=1168.

Didi-Huberman, Georges. L'image survivante - Histoire de l'art au temps des fantômes selon Aby Warburg. Paris: éditions de Minuit, 2002.

—-. Before the Image, Before Time: The Sovereignty of Anachronism, Trans. Peter Mason. 2008.

Foucault, Michel. The Order of Things. New York: Routledge, 2002.

Fulcanelli. The Dwellings of the Philosophers. www.cista.net/Houses/. Trans. Brigitte Donvez and Lionel Perrin.

Garin, Eugenio. Moyen âge et Renaissance. Paris: Gallimard, 1969.

Gombrich, Ernst. Art and Illusion; A Study in the Psychology of Pictorial Representation. New York: Pantheon, 1965.

Habib, André. "L'œil détaillé." Hors-Champ (2002).

Hudrisier, Henri. « Cicéron aurait-il préconisé le cédérom dans De oratore? » Nouvelles technologies et arts de la mémoire. Paris: éditions 00h00, 2002.

Khayyam, Omar. The Sufistic Quatrains of Omar Khayyam. Trans. Edward Fitzgerald, Edward Henry Whinfield, and J. B. Nicolas. www.gutenberg.org/files/38511/38511-h/38511-h.htm.

Kircher, Athanasius. Ars Magna Lucis et Umbrae. 1646.

Kramer, Robert. Cinémaginaire. 11 (May 2001).

Leibniz, Gottfried Wilhem. The Monadology. Trans. Robert Latta. philosophy.eserver.org/leibniz-monadology.txt

—-. Drôle de pensée touchant une nouvelle sorte de représentation, English trans. Helmar Schramm, Ludger Schwarte and Jan Lazardzig eds., Collection, Laboratory, Theater: Scenes of Knowledge in the 17th Century. Berlin: Walter de Gruyter, 2005, 271.

Liandrat-Guigues, Suzanne. Esthétique du mouvement cinématographique. Paris: Klincksieck, 2005.

Llull, Ramon. Ars Brevis. Pisa, 1308.

Malraux, André. Esquisse d'une psychologie du cinéma. Paris: Nouveau Monde éditions, 2003.

Marker, Chris. Immemory. Les instants vidéo numériques et poétiques. http://www.instantsvideo.com/archives/pmb/opac_css/index.php?lvl=notice_display&id=62

—-. Immemory. Dérives.tv 1997. http://www.derives.tv/Immemory

Marot, Sébastien. L'art de la mémoire, le territoire et l'architecture. Paris: Editions de la Villette, 2010.

Maulpoix, Jean-Michel. « L'Art de la Mémoire. » Jean-Michel Maulpoix & Cie www.maulpoix.net/memoire.html.

Michaud, Philippe Alain. Aby Warburg et l'image en mouvement. Paris: Macula, 1998.

Mondzain, Marie-José. Image, icône, économie: Les sources byzantines de l'imaginaire contemporain. Paris: Seuil, 1996.

—-. interview with Michaela Fiserova. Sens Public, 2007.

Montesse, Alain. Cinémaginaire 3. (May 1993).

—-. Nouvelles technologies et arts de la mémoire. Paris: éditions 00h00, 2002.

—-. « nT@M. » écrit-image-oral et nouvelles technologies, Jussieu, Paris, 2002

—-. « Arts de la mémoire en ligne. » colloquium Image et Mémoire, GrIMH Lyon 21-23 Nov. 2002, alain.montesse.voila.net.

Paz, Octavio. in André Breton, L'Art magique - une histoire de l'art. Paris: Phébus, 1991.

Pico della Mirandola, Giovanni. 900 Philosophical, Cabalistic and Theological Conclusions. in Syncretism in the West: Pico's 900 Theses. ed Stephen A. Farmer. Tempe Arizona: MRTS, 1998.

Rhetorica ad Herennium. Trans. Harry Caplan. London: Heinemann; Cambridge: Harvard UP, 1954.

Rieusset-Lemarié, Isabelle. « Des palais de mémoire aux paysages virtuels. » Les enjeux du paysage. Brussels: Ousia, 1997.

Ruiz, Raúl. Poetics of Cinema 1, Miscellanies. Trans. Brian Holmes. Paris: éditions Dis Voir, 1995.

—-. Poetics of Cinema 2. Trans. Carlos Morreo. Paris: éditions Dis Voir, 2007.

—-. « Du jour au lendemain » France Culture, May 22, 1995.

Schefer, Jean-Louis. Du monde et du mouvement des images. Paris: Cahiers du Cinéma, 1997.

Serres, Michel. The Five Senses: A Philosophy of Mingled Bodies. Trans. Margaret Sankey and Peter Cowley. New York: Bloomsbury Academic, 2016.

Severi, Carlo. « Anthropologie et histoire des arts de la mémoire. » Art, Rituel, Mémoire. 17 Mar. 2009, art.rituel.memoire.free.fr/?m=200903

Spence, Jonathan D. The Memory Palace of Matteo Ricci. New York: Viking-Penguin, 1984.

Stoïchita, Victor I. L'instauration du tableau. diss. Sorbonne, 1989, Geneva: Droz, 2003.

Trottein, Serge. « La Naissance de l'iconologie. » Daniel Arasse et al., Symboles de la Renaissance. vol. 2 Paris: Presses de l'École Normale Supérieure, 1982.

Vasari, Giorgio. Lives of the Most Eminent Painters, Sculptors, and Architects, from Cimabue to Our Times. 1550.

Vico, Giambattista. La science nouvelle. (1725) trans. Christina Trivulzio. Paris: Gallimard, 1993.

Vidal, Jordi. Traité du combat moderne - films et fictions de Stanley Kubrick. Paris: Allia, 2005.

von Sternberg, Joseph. Souvenirs d'un montreur d'ombres. Paris: Robert Laffont, 1966.

Warburg, Aby. Mnemosyne Atlas.

---. La naissance de vénus & le Printemps de Sandro Botticelli - études des représentations de l'antiquité dans la première Renaissance italienne. Paris: éditions Allia, 2007.

---. Miroirs de faille — à Rome avec Giordano Bruno et Edouard Manet, 1928-29, Paris: Les Presses du réel, 2011.

Yates, Frances Amelia. The Art of Memory. London: Routledge and Kegan Paul, 1966.

Printed by
Petro ofsetas"
Lithuania
europe

Septemberi 2016